IS THERE
A MEASURE
ON EARTH?

IS THERE

A MEASURE

ON EARTH?

Foundations for a

Nonmetaphysical

Ethics

WERNER MARX

Translated by Thomas J. Nenon
and Reginald Lilly

THE UNIVERSITY OF CHICAGO PRESS
CHICAGO & LONDON

WERNER MARX is professor emeritus at the University of Freiburg and a former professor at the New School for Social Research. Among his many books are *Heidegger and the Tradition; Hegel's "Phenomenology of Spirit"; Reason and World; The Philosophy of F. W. J. Schelling;* and *Introduction to Aristotle's Theory of Being.*

The University of Chicago Press, Chicago 60637
The University of Chicago Press, Ltd., London
© 1987 by The University of Chicago
All rights reserved. Published 1987
Printed in the United States of America

96 95 94 93 92 91 90 89 88 87   54321

This work was originally published as *Gibt es auf Erden ein Maß? Grundbestimmungen einer nichtmetaphysischen Ethik,* © Felix Meiner Verlag, Hamburg, 1983

LIBRARY OF CONGRESS CATALOGING-IN-PUBLICATION DATA

Marx, Werner.
  Is there a measure on earth?

  Translation of: Gibt es auf Erden ein Mass?
  Bibliography: p.
  Includes index.
  1. Heidegger, Martin, 1889–1976—Contributions in ethics. 2. Ethics, Modern—20th century. I. Title.
B3279.H49M313 1987   171'.2   86-24894
ISBN 0-226-50921-4

For Hilde

Die Himmlischen aber, die immer gut sind, alles zumal, wie Reiche,
haben diese Tugend und Freude. Der Mensch darf das nachahmen. Darf,
wenn lauter Mühe das Leben, ein Mensch aufschauen und sagen: so will
ich auch seyn? Ja. So lange die Freundlichkeit noch am Herzen, die Reine,
dauert, misset nicht unglücklich der Mensch sich mit der Gottheit. Ist
unbekannt Gott? Ist er offenbar wie der Himmel? Dieses glaub' ich eher.
Der Menschen Maas ists. Voll Verdienst, doch dichterisch wohnet der
Mensch auf dieser Erde. Doch reiner ist nicht der Schatten der Nacht mit
den Sternen, wenn ich so sagen könnte, als der Mensch, der heißet ein
Bild der Gottheit.

Giebt es auf Erden ein Maaß? Es giebt keines.

But the Heavenly, who are always good, all things at once, like the rich,
have these, virtue and pleasure. This men may imitate. May, when life is
all hardship, may a man look up and say: I too would like to resemble
these? Yes. As long as kindliness, which is pure, remains in his heart, not
unhappily a man may compare himself with the divinity. Is God unknown? Is He manifest as the sky? This rather I believe. It is the measure
of man. Full of acquirements, but poetically, man dwells on this earth.
But the darkness of night with all the stars is not purer, if I could put it
like that, than man, who is called the image of God.

Is there a measure on earth? There is none.

Friedrich Hölderlin, "In lieblicher Bläue," translated by Michael Hamburger as
"In Lovely Blueness" in *Friedrich Hölderlin: Poems and Fragments* (Cambridge:
Cambridge University Press, 1980).

Contents

Translators' Note

All references to Heidegger, Hegel, and Schelling are given in parentheses immediately following the quotation. Although the translations of these quotations have been reviewed and often retranslated for this edition, the page number of the published translation has been listed in italics wherever a translation is available unless the English edition is bilingual or lists the page numbers of the original in the margins.

The following editions and translations of Heidegger's works were used:

Erläuterungen zu Hölderlin's Dichtung (Erl). 2d ed. Frankfurt am Main: Klostermann, 1952.
Gelassenheit (Gel). 5th ed. Pfullingen: Neske, 1977. Translated by J. Anderson and E. Freund as *Discourse on Thinking.* New York: Harper & Row, 1966.
Holzwege (Hw). 3d ed. Frankfurt am Main: Klostermann, 1954. Pp. 7–69 translated by D. Hofstadter as "The Origin of the Work of Art" in *Basic Writings;* pp. 248–320 translated by D. Hofstadter as "What Are Poets For?" in *Poetry, Language, Thought* (New York: Harper & Row, 1971); pp. 296–373 translated by D. Krell as "The Saying of Anaximander" in *Early Greek Thinking* (New York: Harper & Row, 1975).
"Humanismusbrief" *(HBf).* In *Plato's Lehre von der Wahrheit.* Bern: Francke, 1947. Translated by J. Sallis as "Letter on Humanism" in *Basic Writings.* New York: Harper & Row, 1977.
Der Satz vom Grund (SvG). Pfullingen: Neske, 1957.
Schellings Abhandlung über das Wesen der menschliche Freiheit (SK). Tübingen: Niemeyer, 1971. Translated by J. Stammbaugh as *Schel-*

ling's Treatise on the Essense of Human Freedom. Columbus: Ohio
University Press, 1985.

Sein und Zeit (SuZ). 6th ed. Tübingen: Niemeyer, 1949. Translated
by J. Macquarrie and E. Robinson as *Being and Time.* London:
SCM Press, 1962.

Die Technik und die Kehre (TuK). Pfullingen: Neske, 1962. Pp. 5–36
translated by W. Lovitt as "The Question Concerning Technology" in *Basic Writings;* pp. 37–47 translated by W. Lovitt as "The
Turning" in *The Question Concerning Technology and Other Essays*
(New York: Harper & Row, 1978).

Unterwegs zur Sprache (UzS). Pfullingen: Neske, 1959. Pp. 9–34
translated by D. Hofstadter as "Language" in *Poetry, Language,
Thought;* all other essays translated by P. Hertz in *On the Way to
Language* (New York: Harper & Row, 1982).

Vier Seminare. Frankfurt am Main: Klostermann, 1977. (Often referred to in the text simply as "the seminar in Le Thor.")

Vorträge und Aufsätze (VA). Pfullingen: Neske, 1954. Pp. 129–44
translated by D. Krell as "What Calls for Thinking?" in *Basic
Writings;* pp. 145–92 translated by D. Hofstadter as "Building,
Dwelling, Thinking" in *Basic Writings;* pp. 163–86 translated
by D. Hofstadter as "The Thing" in *Poetry, Language, Thought;*
pp. 207–82 translated by D. Krell as "Logos," "Moira," and "Aletheia" in *Early Greek Thinking.*

Was heißt Denken? (WhD). Tübingen: Niemeyer, 1954. Translated by
G. Grey and F. Wieck as *What Is Called Thinking?* New York:
Harper & Row, 1968.

Was ist Metaphysik? (WiM). Frankfurt am Main: Klostermann,
1955. Translated by D. Krell as "What Is Metaphysics?" in *Basic
Writings.*

Vom Wesen der Wahrheit (WdW). 6th ed. Frankfurt am Main: Klostermann, 1976. Translated by J. Sallis as "Concerning the Essence of
Truth" in *Basic Writings.*

Vom Wesen des Grundes. 6th ed. Frankfurt am Main: Klostermann,
1973. Translated by T. Malick as *The Essence of Reasons.* Evanston:
Northwestern University Press, 1969.

Zur Sache des Denkens (ZSD). Tübingen: Niemeyer, 1969. Translated
by J. Stammbaugh and F. Capuzzi as *On Time and Being.* New
York: Harper & Row, 1977.

Zur Seinsfrage. Frankfurt am Main: Klostermann, 1956. Translated by W. Kluback and J. Wilde as *The Question of Being.* New York: Twayne, 1958.

Quotations from Schelling were taken from F. W. J. Schelling, *Werke,* edited by M. Schröter (Munich: Beck, 1927). Following the usual practice, however, we have listed the volume and page numbers of the first edition of Schelling's works, edited by K. F. A. Schelling. These page numbers are listed in the margins of the Schröter edition and of the Gutmann translation of *Of Human Freedom* (La Salle, Ill.: Open Court, 1936).

Hegel's *Philosophy of Right* and *Encyclopedia* were quoted by the paragraph numbers that are listed in all German and English editions of these works.

All other works cited are listed in the notes.

We would like to express our gratitude to Dennis Schmidt, David Krell, John Sallis, and William Smith, who typed the manuscript, for their assistance in the preparation of this translation. We also owe a special debt to the author for his careful review of the manuscript and his support throughout all stages of this translation.

Reginald Lilly
Thomas Nenon

Introduction

According to Walter Schulz's outline of "an ethics for our times,"[1] the "ultimate standards" that have always been considered the fundamental ethical categories are the concepts of "good" and "evil."[2] Schulz regards the good to be the "order of social life" that sustains us from the outset and must be protected from deterioration, especially from evil, which he sees as the suspension of order (cf. 720, 723, 727). Accordingly, Schulz understands the "task of ethics as the promotion of order" (ibid., 727ff., 729ff.).

If the "good as a principle of action" lies in order, then the following question arises: Have we not witnessed, for example, and do we not still witness, totalitarian orders which show us that order as such is not an unqualified "good"? Must we not rather ask what measure we use to determine whether that which purports to be the good is indeed good? Must we not also ask what it is that provides us with a motivation for preferring good to evil?

Unlike Schulz, I do not believe that the concepts of "good" and "evil" are the "ultimate" determinants of ethics; the ultimate determinant is rather the concept of "measure." Thus, for example, Schelling saw "divine" love as the measure that enabled man's "universal will" to discover what is good when man takes measure, and evil was seen to be rooted in the fact that the radically egoistic, particular will excludes divine love. And this measure thus provided the motivation for preferring good to evil.

For Hölderlin, the "heavenly beings"—their goodness, virtues, and joy—were "man's measure" [der Menschen Maas] to which humans could look and against which they could measure themselves in order to remain "pure."

In our age, "heavenly beings" still serve as the measure for the faithful, who see themselves as created in the image of God. However, in our predominantly secularized and pluralistic Western world, many are still disquieted and distressed by the loss and withdrawal of a measure that can provide a standard for responsible conduct. Moreover, as this withdrawal continues, the lack of a measure itself is noticed less and less, and this is happening in an age in which modern technology constantly confronts man with new "moral" questions, an age in which technological achievements call into question what has up until now been taken to be man's fixed "nature," an age in which technology has bestowed upon man the awe-inspiring power to inflict irreversible damage upon or even to annihilate himself as a species along with the surrounding natural environment.

Under these circumstances, contemporary philosophy is confronted by the fact that the Judeo-Christian tradition's concept of an ethics concerned with one's fellow man and a corresponding social ethics is of diminishing efficacy. It no longer seems to possess validity in a world that has grown so much larger. This is perhaps the reason why there have been various attempts to propose an ethics independent of religious doctrine. Examples of this are the logic of moral argumentation and ethics based on linguistic analysis; the attempts to reconstruct and rehabilitate practical philosophy; the social theories proposed by "critical theory"; Walter Schulz's previously mentioned concept of an "ethics of responsibility";[3] and, most recently, Hans Jonas's ethics of "extended responsibility," according to which we must anticipate the "collective cumulative technological" effects of our conduct.[4]

One trait common to all these contemporary efforts to establish an ethics is that "heavenly beings" no longer provide absolute standards for them and that they no longer view man as a rational being created in the divine image. Nevertheless, in spite of their insight into the role of passion and other limits on reason and freedom, these standpoints remain oriented upon man's conception of himself as a rational animal and—in the sense given this term in modern philosophy—as a "subject." They also all arrive at their diverse conceptions of ethics by a process of thought whose method is foundational [*begründend*].

However, there have been tendencies in contemporary philosophy toward an "other thinking" in the attempt not only to overcome radically the presuppositions inherent in the traditional metaphysics of reason and light, but also to overcome the idea of man as a rational animal and a subject. The ethics of such religiously oriented philosophers as Rosenzweig, Buber, Ebner, Maritain, Marcel, and Levinas center upon a renaissance of Judeo-Christian neighborly love. There can be hardly any doubt that Heidegger's "other thinking"—already evident in *Being and Time*—is the most radical attempt to deconstruct the metaphysics of reason and light as well as the determinations of substance and subject that have guided modern philosophy. Furthermore, the aim of his "thinking directed to the *Geschick* of Being" is to "surmount" [*verwinden*] metaphysics as a whole.[5] However, it is a well-known fact that Heidegger refused to propose an "ethics" and that in his later philosophy human interactions in general play only a negligible role. The "rescue" from the "supreme danger" to which, in his view, man is exposed by the "essential unfolding of technology" [*Wesende der Technik*][6] consists in a "turning within Being"[7] that would lead man to overcome [*überwinden*] his self-understanding as a rational animal and a subject and to find his way to a "poetic dwelling."

In light of Heidegger's position, how can we justify the fact that we nevertheless confront his thinking with Hölderlin's ethical question, "Is there a measure on earth?" But first of all, why should we even ask this question? I have posed this question because I am convinced that the real task for those engaged in philosophy today is to search for a new foundation for both an ethics concerned with one's fellow man and a social ethics. Such a foundation would provide measures or standards for those who, having lost their faith, are no longer able to find a measure in religious doctrines. A measure must be found that can offer these persons the possibility of *transformation*. As opposed to those who live in the grace of faith and continue to derive their measure from the "heavenly beings," others for whom this avenue is closed continue to live without orientation and desperately seek to discover whether there might not at least be an experience for them "here on earth" that would provide a measure for distinguishing between good and evil and a motivation for preferring good to evil. I would like to emphasize strongly that I am not seeking the foundation for such an ethics from motives directed against the Judeo-Christian tradition or on atheistic grounds. On the contrary, nothing would be more desirable than that this tradition might predominate today, especially in view of the dangers presented by technology and the peril of nuclear war. Is it not, however, our duty to face the fact that these developments have led many to be excluded from the dimension of the holy, the dimension in which only the faithful find a relationship to a divine being? This distress alone is what led me to the question whether it is not perhaps necessary and timely to search for a foundation for an ethics concerned with one's fellow man that might provide standards "on earth" in forms that are not substantially different from the traditional conceptions of love, compassion, and recognition of one's fellow human beings. Such a nonmetaphysical ethics concerned with one's fellow man could therefore be meaningful for the faithful as well. In my opinion, it is only on the basis of these "traditional virtues" that we can find a motive for averting the impending dangers that have been described so vividly and convincingly. Whoever is indifferent to the suffering and misfortune of others living today and is not even capable of acknowledging them will hardly be concerned about generations to come. Ultimately, the destruction of the "nature" of man will not affect him, and it is more than questionable whether such a person, when faced with the prospect of immediate advantages, will even be concerned about the threat of the annihilation of our entire species. A "rescue" from the danger predominant today seems conceivable only if there is a possibility for even those who are no longer able to derive their concept of measure from a heavenly realm to be capable of an experience that would afford them some kind of measure here on earth.

Despite the unreliability inherent in any empirical observation, one can see that the time has come for such an enterprise. One can see that in view of impending dangers, the forms of our Being-with-others seem to be changing in many quarters. Many persons have changed their indifferent comportment toward others as beings that are merely present, and adopted an attitude of solidarity in which they come to treat others as persons with a common feeling for each other. Even if this is not due to the experience dealt with in the following pages, and certainly it does not always stem from religious conviction, the fact that many people are attempting to act responsibly encourages one to inquire into the philosophical basis of an ethics with regard to one's fellow man. Nonetheless, even if I should succeed in presenting such an ethics, this alone would not mean that such an ethics *must* be established, for that would require the further proof that another person, simply because he is another person, has a right to be considered part of my responsibility. That, however, is not the task of the present study, which intends only to demonstrate the possibility of an experience that could clear the way for a transformation in which one would be willing to allow measures of a nonmetaphysical ethics towards one's fellow man to become effective within oneself. The objection that most people will reject this experience and hence will not accept the measure I am delineating cannot prevent us from exhibiting the existence of this *possibility,* for here we are dealing with an experience and with measures that are founded in the essence of human Being as such. From the Socratic question concerning the true world as opposed to the world of appearances, up through Husserl's and Heidegger's conceptions of the "phenomenon" as that which must be uncovered, philosophy has articulated and conceived of matters that have a tendency to withdraw themselves from "true" experiencing. The experience that must be brought to light here is, as we will see, our own mortality; and it is just this experience which, because of its tendency to withdraw itself, is capable of providing the foundation for an ethics concerned with one's fellow man, for this experience makes one willing to traverse a pathway that transforms a person by leading him from concealment into the "truth." This is by no means irreconcilable with the fact that only a few might actually embark upon this pathway.

Let us recall, for instance, Heidegger's description of "authentic" *Dasein.* Even though the purpose of this description is not to found an ethics, it too is based on an experience that only a few have, namely those few in whose "resolute Dasein" anxiety "arises" (*Being and Time,* 344), and who have the "clear courage to face essential anxiety" (*WiM* 47). Likewise, in Judeo-Christian ethics an "original experience" serves as a basis for those few who have been granted divine grace, and yet this ethics has had a tremendous effect on those who are not able to bring about this original experi-

ence by themselves. Thus, the commandment to love one's neighbor demands that it be observed universally. Yet its original realization, which occurs in an "unnatural" departure from a way of life
that is regarded as insufficient, presupposes that the individual is
willing to accept certain obligations and that this willingness arises
as a result of a transformation of one's inmost convictions. As such,
these commandments cannot be taught—in contrast to those
"commandments" that follow from them. In this respect they resemble the experience of mortality, which will be dealt with later;
for as a way of human Being, it is an experience that can only be
generally circumscribed. Nor does this contradict the fact that the
possible effects of these basic commandments can and indeed
should be taught as a canon of commandments and laws so that
they may take on an objective form.

These objections are directed only to the question whether or
not an admittedly uncommon experience can serve as the basic determination for a nonmetaphysical ethics. Since my exclusive interest here is this fundamental determination and the task of this
book is not the concrete development of an ethics, I shall touch
only peripherally on the problems in contemporary thinking that
"rehabilitated" practical philosophy deals with. Thus, I shall not
pursue the various forms in which aporias that surface in the *Meno*
have been dealt with in the history of philosophy; I shall not pursue the problems of ethical intellectualism or of formalism and a
priori ethics. I shall discuss neither the structure of "ethical consciousness" [*sittliches Bewusstsein*] nor the role of the normative in
an ethics that, as will be shown, is based on a different determination of the good and of freedom than that of the tradition; I shall
also refrain from inquiring into whether values are entities.

I shall, however, ask: What are the essential characteristics of a
measure as such, if it is no longer tied to "heavenly beings" as the
absolute sources of normative measures? Must not a philosophy
that inquires into the foundation for an ethics concerning one's fellow man and that is supposed to provide a measure on earth, first
ask whether we must not find another way to conceive of the essence of "measure"?

If the question is whether or not it is possible for a foundation for "man's measure" to be found in an experience here on earth, then it seems proper to direct this question toward that contemporary thinker who has most radically tried to free himself from the presuppositions upon which the traditional conceptions of ethics rest, namely, Martin Heidegger. Although his thinking has not yet been investigated in this regard, it might contain new pathways that could lead to a new view of the essence of measure and disclose a measure that exists "on earth." In view of the grave danger inherent in the increasing erosion of traditional beliefs, I think that we should consider the "results" attained by every sort of thinking and test them to see whether they might not provide a possible answer to this question. However, it will turn out that—both with regard to the new determination of the essence of measure as well as the measure itself—this can be achieved only by taking determinations developed by the later Heidegger and critically thinking them further.

That the results of a philosopher's thinking should be "thought further" [*weitergedacht*] is nothing new in the history of philosophy. The left-wing Hegelians, for instance, thought Hegel's categories further and did so in a direction that contradicted his own intentions. However, any attempt to think Heidegger's determinations further confronts the problem that we are faced here with an "other thinking" that cannot be reenacted without difficulty.

In previous publications, I have characterized the historical situation of those of us engaged in philosophy today: we are "condemned" to think in a realm "between tradition and an other beginning."[8] Reflection upon this situation for present-day philosophy might help reveal why here in Germany only a few have attempted to think Heidegger further. It might at the same time indicate the possible type of hermeneutics required for such further thinking.

To this end, we must first recall the two "sides" that enclose our intermediate realm. One side still adheres to the tradition, the onto-logical metaphysics of light that believes in at least the potential rationality of "reality" and in the human faculties of the intellect and reason, in the determination of Being as substance and/or as subject, and in the essence of man as freedom. This side, which bounds the intermediate realm for contemporary philosophy, is also determined by developments tending toward the dissolution of the tradition. Nietzsche, Marx, and Freud could be mentioned here.

The other side that bounds this "intermediate realm" is characterized by a kind of thinking that strives toward an "other beginning."

How are we to conceive of this intermediate realm between these two sides, the realm in which our philosophy is situated today? Our situation is still determined by the effective history of those meanings that originated with the first of the two sides named above. This appears today in an increasing tendency toward rationalization and the predominance of science and technology in areas that philosophy previously claimed as its own. Psychology, psychiatry, sociology, and scientific anthropology are now the areas that determine the meaning of "reality" and the various kinds of human conduct. And it is also evident in the fact that the other contemporary philosophical movements described above take their point of departure from traditional thinking—in particular from Kant's transcendental philosophy or from Hegel's thought. The effort of the New Left to achieve social emancipation through social theory is just one example here. Generally, one can say that these movements in contemporary philosophy have it easier insofar as no "transformation" in their thinking is demanded of them. They can continue to operate in the traditional manner based on reasons and explanations.

But what about the attempts to approach the other side that bounds the intermediate realm, the "other thinking" that seeks to prepare an "other beginning" for possible human experience? Such an attempt faces serious difficulties of a sort that we will also encounter in the following interpretations and that I wish to address directly. A philosophy that has not undergone the transformation in thinking that Heidegger demands but that nevertheless discovers a sound purpose in the steps that led Heidegger to proceed from transcendental-phenomenological thinking to the kind "after the turn" is a philosophy that takes Heidegger's efforts and many "results" of his "other thinking" in earnest. Such a philosophy cannot then merely try to understand it from the outside, but must also direct questions to it.

If such philosophy convinces us that there is something "apo-

reitic" or even "lacking" in Heidegger's later work, then we find ourselves in a dilemma indeed, because we face the accusation that we
have failed to reach the level of this "other thinking." Yet does not
Hegel scholarship also investigate the *Science of Logic* without having
reached the level of "absolute thinking"? Does not Schelling scholarship also study his positive philosophy without being capable of
the "narrative" method of "free thought"? Moreover, there have
also been various attempts that use a variety of methods to "reconstruct" these traditional thinkers' philosophies. What I am
attempting, however, is something that is more ambitious than
reconstruction.

Precisely because reflection upon the intermediate realm within
which we must pursue philosophy today has led us to a clear realization that we cannot simply immerse ourselves in Heidegger's
"other thinking" without further ado, the question of the opening
section of chapter 1 is, to put it in traditional terms: Where does
the essence of measure for the onto-theological tradition and for
our secular world lie today? We must attempt to determine what
the possible contexts of such a measure are for us. We shall then
examine Heidegger's later works in view of whether or not and in
what sense this question presented itself to Heidegger. The traditional thinking employed in this section thus concludes that, in any
case, Heidegger's other thinking did not present a measure endowed
with traditional features. Thus, in pursuit of our goal of conceiving a nonmetaphysical ethics concerning one's fellow man, and in
order to seek the fundamental nonmetaphysical determination
that served as a measure for Heidegger himself, the third and
fourth sections of chapter 1 are devoted to the transition into this
other thinking, as the other side that bounds our intermediate
realm. We will discover this point of transition in Heidegger's determination of the experience of death. Proceeding from the basic
matter at issue here, in particular by way of a phenomenological
description, I shall sketch the transition from the ontologically
understood attunement [*Gestimmtheit*]⁹ of unsettling dread to the
attunement of the healing power as the foundation for an ethics
concerned with one's fellow man that can provide measures "on
earth."

Chapter 2 is based on an interpretation of Heidegger's "Conversation on a Country Path." In thinking Heidegger further, it secures the "sphere" for this disclosure of measure. This sphere is the openness, "the clearing," insofar as, in contrast to Heidegger's view of the occurrence of truth, these are not codetermined by concealment and errancy.

Chapter 3 does not accept unconditionally Heidegger's determination of death, but rather thinks it further by demonstrating how death, as a "third force," mediates between Being and Nothing and by showing how it extends into *Dasein's* experience to turn man into a "mortal," how it awakens man from his indifference toward others and makes him responsive to the notion of measure contained in the love of others so that his comprehension of himself as a rational animal and as a self may be overcome.

Chapter 4 attempts to clarify the essential relationship between death and language, which, as Heidegger himself once wrote, remained "unthought." Chapter 5 subsequently inquires into whether or not and wherein thinking directed to the *Geschick* of Being takes its measure, and the final chapter explicates Heidegger's determination of a measure for poetry. His interpretation of Hölderlin's poem "In Lovely Blueness"—which I also take as my point of departure—provides another opportunity to think Heidegger further in order to bring my own questions into sharper focus.

The questions I am addressing to Heidegger in this study were already of interest to me during my years of emigration when I taught on the graduate faculty of the New School for Social Research in New York. In the final chapter of *Heidegger and the Tradition,* the book I wrote there, I said that Heidegger's determinations must be "thought further" in numerous concrete areas. In the foreword to the second German edition[10] I remarked that, in contrast to efforts in other countries, there has been almost no attempt in Germany to think Heidegger further.[11] In my many years of teaching in Freiburg in the chair associated with Husserl and Heidegger, I have turned to the later Heidegger's nonmetaphysical determinations to inquire whether or not and how they could be "thought further," especially regarding the possibility of a measure that could provide us with a set of standards.[12] I am gratified that at the end of my academic path, I can demonstrate that even such thinking that was intended as a radical departure from traditional "values" can be thought further to possibilities of experience that lead back to these values—that there is a positive answer to Hölderlin's question, "Is there a measure on Earth?" and that this answer can provide at least the possibility of a reference point for those who feel distress over the lack of a measure today.

I would like to thank those who have helped me in preparing the manuscript of this book, in particular, Hans-Reiner Sepp, who was also responsible for the indexes.

ONE

Is There a Measure on Earth? The Measure for Responsible Action

For Hölderlin, it was the "Heavenly," those who are "always good" and possess "virtue and joy," that man "may imitate." For they are "the measure of man" [*der Menschen Maas*]. And it was self-evident to him that man "is called the image of God." His question was whether or not there is a measure on earth; his answer was no.

Nor did Hölderlin's philosophical friends, Hegel and Schelling, question the assumption of the "Heavenly," God as the absolute, the source of measures. Nor did they question that His essence was the measure for men in their determination of measure and that man was "the image of God." These philosophers were just as indubitably convinced that, because man is an image of God, his essence and, in particular, his freedom must be so determined that man can derive his measure for practical and ethical orientation on earth from this absolute.

God still serves as the source of measures for religious faith in our day. But many are distressed over the loss and withdrawal of measures; and increasingly even lack of a measure is no longer noticed by those who wish to act responsibly. This is the chief characteristic of the increasing predominance of nihilism in the present age, which is a result of the increasing estrangement and loss of meaning in the Western world—something that Nietzsche foresaw and that has been most radically articulated in Sartre's experience of existence. This is the ongoing result of the unheard-of achievements attained by modern technology, which attacks with increasing vehemence what has been held to be the "nature" of man and places man in danger of destroying the entire human race.

Is it not then philosophy's most urgent task to inquire into the foundation of an ethics concerned with one's fellow man, i.e., to seek a measure that can provide a means for distinguishing between good and evil and furnish a motivation for preferring good to evil?

Of course in ancient times the metaphysical tradition had already posed and attempted to answer the question of a measure; one might recall, for example, Plato's "Idea of the Good" and Aristotle's response to this doctrine. This question was also the basis for the ethics proposed by Western Christian philosophers, who employed foundational thinking in determining God as that Being who, as *causa sui,* is the absolute from which we draw our concept of measure. Accordingly, for Hegel, at the end of this tradition, the substance of ethical life was still the absolute truth inherent in the absolute as determined in a Christian, Protestant tradition. All these philosophers shared Hölderlin's view that there is no measure on earth.

Yet already in the past century such thinkers as Feuerbach, Marx, and Nietzsche expressed doubts about the presuppositions involved in the metaphysical determinations of an absolute that can serve as a measure. To an increasing degree, the assumption made in the metaphysics of light, namely, that reason can attain, at least potentially, complete supremacy, was called into question; along with it, all thinking based on the categories of "substance" and, in particular, of "subject" was rendered questionable. One tendency in contemporary philosophy has been the attempt to open up other possibilities for human thought and experience by means of an "other thinking" that, in "deconstructing" the presuppositions of rationalistic philosophies, has abandoned the deductive and dialectical methods of foundational metaphysics.

Nonetheless, I would not be giving a true picture of the philosophical situation today if I were to maintain that philosophy is still dominated by this tendency toward a deconstruction of the presuppositions inherent in rationalistic philosophy. Quite to the contrary, there are numerous contemporary enterprises that, in one way or another, still share the traditional presuppositions of rationalistic philosophy. To a great extent, they have led to a loss of interest in nonmetaphysical attempts at an "other thinking"; and this is perhaps one reason why the question has not previously been posed as to whether or not one can proceed from Heidegger's basic determinations in order to propose a "nonmetaphysical ethics." Another reason is the fact that many are not able to reenact his "other thinking" themselves and yet are not longer willing simply to imitate Heidegger, as was so common just a short time ago.

However, is a position that now simply attempts to ignore this "other thinking" and its results appropriate to our "hermeneutic situation"? Can we simply make something disappear once it has occurred in the history of thought? Whether we realize it or not, Heidegger's "other thinking" has raised us to a new level of reflection that we must take into account even where we are not able to reenact such thinking ourselves. It cannot be denied that this results in enormous difficulties, but we must try to recognize and bear them as such. It could be that, for the reasons indicated in the Introdution, we are entitled and even obligated to philosophize in a realm "between tradition and an other beginning," and this implies that we must at least try to come closer to Heidegger's "other thinking"—even if we can do so only from our own perspective, which is still determined by the tradition and the meanings it entails. We must remain open to the question of whether or not the answers that this thinking can give us might not disclose meanings that could be significant for our thinking today.

For this reason as well as those indicated in the Introduction, in this study I shall direct my question, "Is there a measure on earth?" to Heidegger's nonmetaphysical thinking and its basic nonmetaphysical determinations. I do so not merely out of historical interest, but rather because our desperate situation today means that we cannot afford to ignore the possibilities inherent in such thought or its "results," for they might provide an answer to this question that could not be found within the tradition alone. And in my view, this is also why we are justified in not merely being content with the basic nonmetaphysical determinations as Heidegger presented them, but rather in proceeding to think them still further than he did himself. Therefore, my intention is to take Heidegger's basic determinations and expose the real content underlying them in order to see whether there might not be other possibilities inherent within them that Heidegger failed to notice. I thereby claim neither to reenact this "other thinking" myself nor to imitate it. Although such "thinking further" [*Weiterdenken*] might discover possibilities that are alien to Heidegger's own efforts, this is a risk I consciously take. Heidegger justified his own enterprise by pointing out that what is at stake is nothing less than "saving" mankind from the "supreme danger" confronting us today. If such thinking further can point out possibilities that could be our "rescue" in a genuine sense, even though Heidegger himself failed to notice them, then this would at least do justice to Heidegger's own purposes.

In order to respond consciously to our "hermeneutic situation" today and in order to find a way to approach Heidegger's basic determinations, this study must take a roundabout route in addressing the question "Is there a measure on earth?" to his later writings. It is unavoidable that in the first section we must clarify the question about what constitutes the essence of a measure for us today. Proceeding from the assumption that the limits of our understanding today are still determined by traditional meanings, but that these, having been secularized, now point in a new direction, we shall turn to Schelling's traditional conception and derive the essential traits of a measure from his philosophy.

In section 2 I shall proceed from this traditional meaning of a measure and inquire into whether the later Heidegger's use of the term "measure" at various stages stemmed from this meaning or whether his nonmetaphysical determinations were founded upon another sense of the essence of a measure that he himself did not make explicit. The reader who is less interested in this second, (which is still introductory), i.e., in the question whether or not Heidegger's thinking contains a measure for responsible action, can proceed directly to the core of this study in sections 3 and 4. There I take Heidegger's determination of the experience of death as my point of departure in order to present my outline of a nonmetaphysical ethics concerned with one's fellow man.

In section 3 I shall develop this conception by "thinking further" one of Heidegger's basic nonmetaphysical determinations. It will be seen that there is a "measure" with other essential traits, namely, the "healing power" [*das Heilende*],[1] which as such and in the form in which it appears as love of neighbor, compassion, and recognition of others contains secularized religious determinations of meaning, but that nevertheless can be experienced "here on earth."

Section 4 deals with the question of what good and evil mean in light of the essence of measure if it is conceived of differently than it is in the tradition, as well as with the meaning and role of "freedom."

1. The Traditional, Essential Traits and the Content of a Measure

The task of demonstrating the meaning or the essential traits of the determination "measure," upon which the limits of our understanding today are ostensibly based, can be properly fulfilled only by means of a comprehensive intentional analysis. However, this cannot be achieved in conjunction with the questions dealt with here. Assuming that our contemporary understanding of measure still contains certain residual traditional meanings, we shall take a shorter, though not completely satisfactory route: we shall turn to one comprehensive conception taken from the history of metaphysics, a conception whose categories still rest on the traditional understanding of measure and yet whose problematic points to tendencies that are pertinent to us today. We shall derive the meaning and essential traits of a measure from it, fully conscious of the fact that this meaning and these traits still determine our contemporary understanding of measure, but that they nevertheless must make way for a different comprehension of measure made necessary by the changes in our situation.

The Onto-theological Position: Schelling

I have intentionally chosen a conception that proceeds, with the same apparent certainty as Hölderlin's, from the assumption that the "Heavenly" are the "measure of man" and that man "is called the image of God." One of the reasons I shall attempt to illustrate Schelling's view of the meaning of measure is because the problems dealt with in his *Inquiries into the Essence of Human Freedom* manifest certain tendencies that call into question the traditional meaning of a measure and were thus the occasion to try once again to stabilize it.[2] And above all, I shall address myself to Schelling because

Heidegger himself dealt with Schelling's *Inquiries* in his lecture of 1936 and in a seminar in 1941, as well as in his seminar notes.

Accordingly, I intend to proceed by presenting the categorial structure of the *Inquiries* so that one can recognize which meaning or essential traits of a measure provide the foundation for this work. The first fact to be noted is that in the *Inquiries*, just as in every onto-theological conception of metaphysics that provides the foundation for an "ethics," there is a higher categorial level determining the Being of God the Creator. As the "primary" level, this level serves as a "measure" for the "subordinate" categorial level that determines the creature that is fashioned in the divine image. This twofold structure is decisive for the traditional view of measure, as can be seen by the fact that the meaning of a measure must change as soon as this twofold structure no longer holds.

The *Inquiries*, even with their Christological tendencies towards the higher level that provides measures, are intentionally anthropological ("in order to bring us closer to God"), i.e., this level is defined in terms derived from the subordinate level. God's character as absolute in his "absolute freedom," his "absolute reason," and, above all, his "absolute will" taken as "the willing of divine love," is the decisive measure for man, for it serves as a point of orientation for man throughout the ongoing history of redemption, shows him the difference between good and evil, and provides a motivation for preferring good to evil.

The categories just named are all expressions of the "ideal principle" in God. Correspondingly, from whatever man takes his measure, the categories of the subordinate level are also an expression of an ideal principle in man. This holds for his "derivative" absolute freedom, his intellect, his reason, and his universal will, which, when it is in accord with the particular will, is able to imitate "divine love."

However, one of the basic problems in mysticism and German Romanticism, the contexts in which the *Inquiries* were composed, is that the higher categorial level that determines God's being is dominated not only by an "ideal," but also by a "real" principle as well; and the same is true of the subordinate level that determines creatures modeled after the divine image.

God is not "pure" spirit and "pure" reason. Rather, he has, in an "unconscious longing," emerged from a "dark ground" through "self-contraction," and has his foundation and nature in this ground. Thus, the fact that there is a principle of darkness in God leads to difficulties in maintaining the absoluteness of divine Being as a possible point of orientation for man. Furthermore, because there is also a real principle that similarly predominates in man's essence, it is also necessary to conceive of a real foundation for man's reason. Above all, man's freedom, as we shall see more clearly later, must be determined as "real" freedom for both good *and* evil, for the existence of evil increasingly threatens to intrude into the "well-ordered" [*heile*] world. This reality is to be viewed not only Christologically as sin in the first and second creation, but also as a "positive force in Being." What meaning can the normative measure that provides an absolute orientation for man have if there is a "principle of darkness" in God's essence? How can human freedom as the universal will imitate this divine love if evil essentially enters into this dimension of freedom and can determine it? The most pressing question with regard to the problems we are dealing with is how Schelling was able to rescue the traditional meaning of measure in face of these threats. For he was indeed able to rescue this meaning by means of a special sort of turn in his *Theodicy* and by employing the idea of a history of salvation.

There is no need here to give a detailed presentation of the way that Schelling conceived of a "dark ground" that was indeed created by God and belongs to him but lies outside of his absoluteness. This principle was where the first creation began and constitutes the real basis for the divine personhood. Schelling explains that evil, stemming as it does from its own principle, is a "possibility" in its "reality" only because of the solicitation of man. Man, however, if cognizant of the final purpose in the history of salvation, can resist this solicitation because he has freed himself for goodness by taking up the struggle against evil within the "moral dimension" of freedom. The "will of divine love" prevails as a possible point of orientation for mankind even where evil threatens to gain the upper hand because it is able to persevere throughout the history of salvation as "self-same" and because it continually serves as a marker throughout the history of salvation insofar as it is "univocal" and "manifest." Even if only implicitly, the further essential traits of the "self-same," the "manifest," and the "univocal" are present in the very imperilment of the meaning of measure as such.

From Schelling's philosophy we can now derive the following essential traits of a measure according to the onto-theological view: A measure is a "normative standard" that as such contains the demand of an "ought." As something already valid prior to any derivation of measure, its mode of Being is one of "transcendence." At the same time, it has the "power" to determine man "immanently," and herein lies the decisive significance of a measure, its "binding obligation." It also has the power to endure as "self-same" in various situations and thus has the traits of being "manifest" and "univocal."

The Secularized Version of the Traditional Position

Can we say that these determinations of the meaning of a measure have become so much a part of our understanding of things that they still have unqualified validity for us today? In our secularized age, religious ideas based on the Bible have lost most of their effectiveness. Not everyone still believes that there is a divine creator as an absolute measure and that God created man in His image and likeness. Even fewer believe that evil can be eliminated through recourse to the idea of a history of salvation now that the destructive power of evil has become completely apparent in two world wars and the reign of totalitarian regimes, and now that the predominance of technology has opened up new possibilities for spiritual corruption. For traditional ethics, the structure of the higher categorical level is determined by a divine Creator who is the source of measure. But if this level is no longer readily acceptable within the boundaries of our understanding today, and if the "will of divine love" is no longer valid within the categorical level of mere creatures, then must we not ask whether the traditional, essential traits of measure mentioned above can still hold for us?

Are there any measures for us today that possess the traits listed above? It seems that measures are no longer valid in the traditional sense of the "true," the "good," and the "beautiful." But do not measures still exist, even if only as secularized versions of the forms

of ethics concerned with one's fellow man that have been handed
down to us in the Judeo-Christian tradition? These include love of
neighbor, compassion, and justice, although given the nihilism pre-
vailing today these may be dismissed as mere "romanticism."

For everything that follows, it is important to note that in place
of an extensive phenomenological description, I shall merely clarify what I mean by love, compassion, and recognition of others and
state why I speak of them as measures by attributing to them the
essential traits derived above.

Whenever I speak here or later of "love," I also mean its "weaker"
forms of fraternity, friendship, and social solidarity. Wherever I
speak of compassion, I mean every sort of kindness toward and
concern for others. I will also deal with the possibilities of for-
giveness and justice as instances of "recognizing others" although I
cannot go into the problem of legal "recognition" in general or the
problems of justice that are part of a social ethics. My concern
is rather the essential ontological character of "attunements" [*Ge-
stimmtheiten*], which in their manifold and ambiguous facets play
a role in the matters which form the basis for these traditional
determinations.

From ancient times up until the present, philosophers have determined the essence of love in a number of different ways.[3] Here,
however, I am not referring to the philosophical determinations of
love. I mean love in its factuality; for it is only *post factum* that it is
given philosophical and psychological determinations. Love possesses the traits of a measure conceived of in a traditional, "metaphysical" fashion. For those who love, it is "absolutely" valid, it is
something that they share "over and above" their individuality, and
in this sense it is a "transcendent" normative standard for them.
Nonetheless, everyone who loves experiences it as "immanent"
within himself. For love is a power that permeates those who love
and binds them by bestowing on them an obligation that they experience without prior reflection. In its various forms, the power of
love remains the "same." For those who love, it is "manifest" and
provides them with a "univocal" orientation vis-à-vis good and
evil; love as a measure provides a motivation for preferring the
good, which is filled with love, to evil, in which love is lacking.

Though love is possible only in "smaller groups," compassion can be present in larger groups that may even remain anonymous.[4] For those who are filled with compassion, compassion is "absolutely" valid. It obtains as a "transcendent" normative standard even though compassion, as experienced by those who feel it, is something "immanent." It is constantly binding for the compassionate as something that is the "same" in a variety of possible personal and public situations, for example in times of war or persecution. The obligating power of compassion instigates actions without any further reflection whatsoever. As such, compassion is something that is "manifest" and thus "univocal." It therefore provides a way to distinguish between good and evil as well as a motivation for preferring good to evil.

Recognition of others is "absolute," and for those who recognize one another it is a "transcendent" normative standard that they nonetheless experience "immanently" whenever they grant others recognition as a matter of course.[5] Such recognition is always the "same" for them, whether it concerns friendship, one's family, civil or private institutions, or whatever, and regardless of the various justifications given for it. Once one has seen the "obligatory" character inherent in this form of "intersubjectivity," then it works as a binding power which as such is manifest and univocal and thus can guide a person without further reflection and provide him with a means to distinguish between good and evil and give him a motivation for preferring good to evil.

We then come to the conclusion that, strangely enough, these measures, which have their origins in the onto-theological tradition, still seem to be valid. However, since their legitimation is derived from a belief in "heavenly powers," these measures have lost much of their effectiveness today; they have fallen into ruin.

For anyone engaging in philosophy "between the tradition and an other beginning," the question, then, is whether it is not the task of philosophy to proceed beyond these ruinous determinations of measure according to the traditional view. We must ask whether there might not be another kind of thinking than traditional foundational thought, whether there might not be a different kind of thinking—an "other thinking"—that has already been able to conceive of a different sort of measure with different essential traits. Even if this has not yet come about, then we must still ask whether we cannot bring to light the issue with which this line of thought is concerned and then try to "think further" in this direction. In this particular case, I would like to address these questions to Martin Heidegger's thinking.

2. Heidegger and the Question of a Measure for Responsible Action

These presuppositions regarding God's absoluteness and man's likeness to God, from whom man derives his measures, were presuppositions that Schelling took for granted. Looking back on them, we can now contrast them with the other aspect of the situation which is the context of our thinking. Taking this side of our situation into account, we must seek a new philosophical response to Hölderlin's question, "Is there a measure on earth?" a question to which he and his philosophical contemporaries gave such a radically negative response. How can we answer this question if those who have no religious ties can no longer presuppose that heavenly powers provide all measures and that the essence of man in the act of determining measures consists in his likeness to God? How do we answer it if the reality of evil can no longer be glossed over by reference to the history of salvation? How can philosophy provide an answer to this question for those who try to act responsibly today, for those who still find some meaning in the terms "good" and "evil," and who claim to have a motive for preferring good to evil?

It seems that this urgent question must have confronted Martin Heidegger and that we should be able to find an answer to it in his later writings, since in those writings he took up the task of combatting nihilism. These writings were composed in the period prior to the catastrophe of World War II, during the war, and in the phase shortly following, i.e., in a time when the desperation over the apparent lack of a measure that his contemporaries could have used to orient themselves climaxed in the cry of those who still held their religious faith: "Where was God in Auschwitz?"

The Question Not Raised in the Commentary on Schelling

In the thirties, Heidegger addressed himself to Schelling's *Inquiries into the Nature of Human Freedom*. It would then seem plausible to suppose that in this work the same questions confronted him that concern us, the questions of whether or not there is a measure and how it can be thought of as providing a point of orientation, the question of how we can think about the meaning of good and evil and conceive of the essence of man and especially of man's freedom now that many no longer share Schelling's Christological presuppositions. Did Heidegger truly confront these questions or is there something "lacking" here as there is in his later statements, something that would lead us to think further those basic determinations that he arrived at in his "nonmetaphysical" thinking? There can be no doubt that, in Schelling, Heidegger discovered something of a "transition" to present-day philosophy, but that he nevertheless tried to separate it from its Christological framework and subordinate it to the intentions involved in his own work. However, what thereby falls by the wayside is Schelling's desperate attempt to conceive of the possibility of evil as something only "indirectly" attributable to God and to locate its actuality in its appearance within the realm of human freedom as a moral dimension. Heidegger declares from the very outset that his intention is to deal with evil "not from the perspective of simple morality, but from the perspective of ontological and theological questions" (*SK* 117, *97*). For "the scope of ethics does not suffice if one wants to comprehend evil" (ibid., 176, *146*). He therefore intentionally abstracts from Schelling's view of evil, according to which evil is not only a positive force in Being but also a "sin." "We shall not inquire into the question of evil in the form of sin," Heidegger writes, "but with regard to the essence and truth of Being." This point is decisive.

Schelling carefully distinguished between the absolute measure for orientation in ethical conduct and divine Being as a whole in which there is the power of darkness. This power, however, is not binding for freedom and is therefore not the origin of evil. Schelling excluded evil from the sphere of the absolute because he wanted to retain the purity of the divine absolute as that realm which provides measures for the "moral dimension of human freedom." Heidegger, in contrast, tends to obliterate this distinction; he ignores this ontological duality by explicitly stating that evil is relevant for him only "in view of the essence and truth of Being." No extensive demonstration is necessary here to show that Heidegger's sole concern in his interpretation of the *Inquiries* was his view of the "truth of Being," for he openly declares that his commentary on Schelling is "intentionally one-sided in view of the mainstream of philosophy, the question of Being" (cf. ibid., 176, *146;* 128, *106–7*). It was from this vantage that he saw the inner possibility of evil and considered the "differentiation" between ground and existence that makes this possible as the "jointure of Being" [*Seinsfüge*], as the "fundamental arrangement of jointures [*Grundgefüge*] made by that entity that stands on its own." For this reason, it is necessary that the "demonstration of how the possibility of evil is made possible must proceed from the jointure of Being, allowing this possibility to arise" (ibid., 144, *120*). And though Heidegger himself assembled a list of traditional concepts of freedom (cf. ibid., 106, *88*), he took the problem of freedom to be a fundamental determination of Being from the very outset. The concept of freedom is said to have "reality" if being free as a way of Being belongs to the essence and the essential ground of Being. Therefore freedom is thought of not as an "addition and attribute of the human will, but rather as the essence of authentic Being, as the essence of the ground for beings as a whole" (ibid., 11, *9*). By contrast, according to my interpretation, the decisive point in Schelling's treatise lies in the fact that freedom is conceived of as a moral dimension in which good *and* evil appear and that the struggle between them occurs in light of the absolute measure. Since the good that is the goal in the history of salvation is the reign of the divine will of love, this is the measure that the responsible agent must take as his standard when attempting to bring his universal will into the "correct relationship" with his particular will. In his commentary on Schelling, Heidegger thus intentionally omitted this sphere of "morality."

The "Letter on Humanism" Contains No Measure for
Responsible Action

In order to understand why this is so, one should recall that the
early Heidegger was part of a movement that, under the influence
of Nietzsche and Kierkegaard, opposed "Platonism" and every sort
of "essentialism." Sartre even included Heidegger in the group of
existentialist thinkers who dealt with the determinations of essence and existence by simply reversing the relationship that had
been handed down to them in the tradition. Although Heidegger
raised strong objections to this view in the "Letter on Humanism"
and made it clear that his determination "ek-sistence" had nothing
to do with the traditional category of "existence," he was nonetheless a radical opponent of Platonism and essentialism just as much
as Sartre (cf. *HB* 64ff., *202ff.; 72ff., 208ff.*). In view of the history
of Being, Heidegger considered Platonism and essentialism to be
characteristic of a falling away from the experiences that the Presocratics had with Being in the "first beginning"; they represent the
beginning of "metaphysics," which "culminates" today in the predominance of the emerging essence of technology. Does this not
imply that our inquiry into measure, in particular into a measure
for responsible action, could be equated with a relapse into metaphysics, into essentialism and Platonism?

However, in his writings at the beginning of the "turn" as well as
in various works from the period thereafter, Heidegger himself
spoke of "measure" and "taking measure" in connection with a
number of different questions. Did he inquire there into the *essence*
of a measure as such and try to determine its traits? Strangely
enough, he did so only peripherally. For instance, he once remarked
that "the essence of a measure is no more a quantum than is the
essence of a number" (ibid., 199, 224); but he provided no fundamental answer to the question of what traits a measure must
possess. Nowhere did he discuss if and how the determination
"measure" is compatible with this basic anti-Platonic and anties-
sentialist position, which he understood as an attempt to surmount metaphysics.

Hence, the question remains whether Heidegger in his own
usage of the term "measure" accepted the meaning its traditional,

metaphysical traits imply, or whether his determinations were to some extent covertly based on a nonmetaphysical essence of measure that resulted from his nonmetaphysical, "other" thinking. In his essay "Poetically Man Dwells . . ." Heidegger analyzed Hölderlin's poem "In Lovely Blueness," which was cited in the Introduction and attempts to determine the measure taken by the poet. In earlier treatments of Hölderlin's poetry (cf. *EHD* 39–40), he also spoke of such a measure. In the "Letter on Humanism," the question concerns a measure for thinking: "Whence does thinking take its measure? What is the law for what it does?" (*HB* 117, 240) But the question still remains: Did Heidegger in his later writings inquire into a measure for responsible action?

In Heidegger's "Letter on Humanism," which is directed against Sartre's lecture "Existentialism Is a Humanism" (Paris, 1946), he reponds to Beaufret's question as to whether and how one can conceive of the relation between ethics and ontology, and when he intended to write an ethics. He observes that ontology and ethics have existed as separate disciplines only since a particular era that began with Plato, and that the question regarding this relationship was superficial in the form in which Sartre had posed it. By contrast, in accordance with the basic meaning of the word *ēthos,* the Presocratics had directed their thought to "man's abode" among the whole array of beings; similarly, Heidegger says that his thinking is concerned with determining "the truth of Being as the primal element of man as one who ek-sists" (109, 335). Such thinking is said to be neither ontology nor ethics; it is supposed to be neither practical nor theoretical; and it occurs "prior to this distinction" (ibid., 109, 235; 111, 237). Heidegger states that Sartre's humanism, by contrast, is metaphysical, for it is conceived "in the forgottenness of the truth of Being" (ibid., 72, 208), just as all humanistic determinations coincide by metaphysically determining the "*humanitas* of the *homo humanus*" in view of a preconceived interpretation concerning the nature of history, the world, and the ground of the world (ibid., 63, 202). What must be done, however, is to think "in service of the truth of Being, but without humanism in the metaphysical sense" (ibid., 104, 231). The task is to think man's eksistence, i.e., his "stance in the clearing of Being" (ibid., 66ff., 204ff.) in an original manner and not simply to suppose that the essence of man lies in his being an *animale rationale* in a Christian or Marxist sense (ibid., 63–64, *201–2*) or a "nature" that must be projected ever anew, as Sartre suggests. The task of thinking, as Heidegger sees it in the "Letter on Humanism," lies solely in letting Being be. Thus he says: "It [thinking] helps build the house of Being, in which the jointure [*Fuge*] of Being in each particular mittance enjoins the essence of man to dwell in the truth of Being" (ibid., 111, *236*). In the passage immediately following, Heidegger quotes the line from Hölderlin's poem "In Lovely Blueness" that I cited at the beginning of this study. The line reads: "full of merit, but poetically, man dwells on this earth." However, he fails to quote the verses that led me to my question concerning the measure and man in his measure-taking. Instead, Heidegger states: "Thinking conducts historical ek-sistence, that is, the *humanitas* of *homo humanus* into the realm of the upsurgence of the hale. Evil appears together with the hale in the clearing of Being. Its essence consists not in something base in human actions, but rather in the evilness of malice. However, both of them, the hale and malice, can reign in Being only insofar as Being itself is in conflict" (ibid., 112, *237*).

In my opinion this is precisely the point where Heidegger responded to Schelling's determination of the ideal and the real. Schelling had thought of them as forces in the "life" of the absolute, God; while Heidegger here thinks of them as belonging to Being, whose "truth" for him consisted in an event of concealing and clearing. It is also important to recall that, while Schelling took care to exclude evil from the dimension of the divine measure in order to be able to secure its absolute validity, according to Heidegger evil appears in the occurrence of Being itself as an occurrence of truth. If we assume that Being, thought of as this occurrence of truth, had the sense of a measure for Heidegger—whether or not this is indeed the case can remain open for the moment—then one important difference would be that, for Schelling, evil (and good) appears within the dimension of human freedom, which, by contrast, is no longer spoken of in the "Letter on Humanism." The more significant difference, however, lies in Heidegger's view that "the hale [*das Heile*] and malice [*Grimm*] reign in Being only insofar as Being itself is in conflict" (ibid.). For Schelling, there is a "conflict" between good and evil only in the "real" concept of freedom precisely because it is a "moral" dimension. The conflict between good and evil results solely from the conflict of whether or not and how the human spirit brings the relationship between the universal and particular wills into a "correct," i.e., good relationship or into an "inverse," i.e., evil one. The correct relationship results only if one establishes one's measure in light of the absolute measure of the divine "will of love."

Why then does Heidegger immediately conclude from the "conflicting character" of Being that the hale appears *as* hale and that malice appears *as* malice in its clearing? We are given no answer to this question. Instead, the passage just cited, according to which Being itself is "in conflict," is followed by a sentence that deals with the "essential" provenance of nihilating [*Wesensherkunft des Nichtens*]. This provenance is said to conceal itself in the conflicting character of Being, and nihilating is not supposed to be "an existing quality of beings," but rather "nihilating reigns in Being itself" (ibid., 113, 237). Put even more pointedly, "Being nihilates—as Being," and "that which nihilates in Being is the essential unfolding of what I call Nothing" (ibid., 114, 238).

The question concerning "that which nihilates" as the "essence of Nothing" and its relationship to Being persists in Heidegger's thought from *Being and Time* and the inaugural lecture "What Is Metaphysics?" up through his final works. Though Heidegger stated in the introduction to *Being and Time* that the sole issue was the question concerning the meaning of Being—later he called it the "truth of Being"—his concern was always just as much the question of the "meaning" of the "truth" of Nothing. We shall not pursue in detail here this aspect of the path his thought took. What is important to realize is that when Heidegger speaks of nihilation and Nothing, he does not mean the *nihil negativum,* and that the various modes of "nihilating," especially nihilating as anxiety, do not occur "outside of being, but rather in Being."

Did Heidegger simply identify the nihilating occurrence, Nothing, and the occurrence of Being? In one of the following chapters I shall, in thinking Heidegger further, try to show that this is not the case for the later Heidegger. Rather for him death—understood, of

course, not as the "decay of the body" but as the "supreme concealment of Being," as the "shelter" [Gebirg][6] of the mystery of unconcealedness in its calling"—mediates between Being and Nothing.
In one of his last courses in Le Thor in 1969, Heidegger formulated
the question as follows: "Being: Nothingness: The Same?" By demonstrating that there is such a mediation, we have answered this
question. In the present context, however, we must address ourselves to a different question. Heidegger showed that the essential
provenance of nihilation, which conceals itself, lies in the conflicting character of Being. Did he thereby intend to show that this conflicting character makes possible the appearance of malice "together with" the hale, so that both of them are forms in which the
nihilating occurrence of Being appears? That would mean that the
hale cannot be without malice nor malice without the hale; and
more importantly, that there is no way to distinguish between
these forces in Being. Is this not also true of Schelling's "real" concept of freedom which, in direct opposition to the tradition, determined freedom as good *and* evil?

This "and," however, means that, although for Schelling both elements appear in human freedom, there is also a measure, the measure of divine love, in light of which the agent measures and therefore knows what is good and hence what is evil. Heidegger, by
contrast, gives no immediate indication how an agent can recognize the difference between the hale and malice within the conflicting occurrence of Being and truth, since that which nihilates comes
to be in Being in the form of malice "together with" the hale.

In the "Letter on Humanism" Heidegger declares, "Being alone
grants the hale its ascent into grace and malice its compulsion to
malignancy" (114, 238).

The further question is how we should think of this "granting."
Assuming instead of an ascension of the hale that malice becomes
compelling—and for Heidegger, this could very well happen because of the conflicting character of Being—how does the agent
really decide that what is motivating him is the hale and not malice?

In response to this question, Heidegger would point out that, according to the determinations developed in the "Letter on Humanism" (77ff., 211), man ek-sists in the clearing as the "truth of

Being," that he therefore "belongs to Being," and that this means that man is capable of listening to Being. He expressly states in this connection that if man "finds his way to an abode in the truth of Being" (ibid., 115, *238–39*), he hears the "assignment of those directives" that proceed "from Being itself" and hence "must become law and rule" for him, whereby "law" "in a more original sense" means the "assignment [*Weisung*] borne in the *Geschick*⁷ of Being," an assignment that is capable of "enjoining man in Being" and therefore of "bearing and binding" him, that can give him "support" [*Halt*] and "shelter" [*Hut*] (cf. ibid., 114–15, *239*).

The question remains: Is there a measure and thus a possibility of taking measure within such Being that is in conflict with itself? Thinking traditionally, we can first ask about measure in the traditional, metaphysical sense developed above, i.e., as an absolute normative standard given prior to and transcendent of all measuring, but that nonetheless is at the same time "immanent" and has the binding force of an obligation, a standard that is furthermore "univocal" and "manifest." The determination "truth of Being" would then be a measure in the same sense as the absolute in the form of divine love was for Schelling. If this were the case, then *Dasein* would only have to listen to the "assignment contained in the *Geschick* of Being" and simply obey it almost "automatically," even if the context of assignment were disastrous and malicious. Such consequences would be diametrically opposed to the meaning of a measure in the traditional sense. This becomes clear as soon as one recalls that Schelling precluded the possibility of evil's intrusion into the realm of the "ethical" not only by holding the absolute free from the "powers of darkness" but also by conceiving of the existence of evil only within the dimension of human freedom, in which it appears together with the good. In the "Letter on Humanism," Heidegger no longer speaks in terms of freedom, sin, guilt, accountability, or responsibility. I will soon show how the issues bound up in the traditional determination of "freedom" came to be neglected in Heidegger's enterprise because they became absorbed into those issues that Heidegger conceived of in the determination "truth." First, however, the negative result of our attempt to view Heidegger's determination "the truth of Being" as a measure in the traditional sense compels us to ask another question. We must inquire whether this determination is not meant as the expression of an "other" essence of a measure that Heidegger "covertly" introduced without himself specifying it as one of the themes of his inquiry.

Is There Any Indication of a Measure in Heidegger's Later Writings, Either in the Traditional or in an "Other" Sense?

The question then is whether or not one can find an "other" determination of the essence of measure in the same way that one can find determinations of "the abode of man's essence in the truth of Being," i.e., man's "ek-sistence," in Heidegger's nonmetaphysical and hence antisubjectivistic thought. As I mentioned above, Heidegger did inquire into the measure for thinking in the "Letter on Humanism." And if one brings into play the determinations Heidegger employed in his later writings, then one can see how human being [*das Menschenwesen*] takes up the claim of Being, its soundless address, as a *Geschick* to thinking to which the thinker's "articulated" [*verlautende*] word responds since it is something directed to that *Geschick*.

It appears that such "responding" to the "claim" [*Anspruch*] of Being would be a "measure" that would not be identical with a measure as thought of in the metaphysical sense described above. It would not be an absolute standard that is "transcendent" and yet "immanent" to man as a "binding force." Rather, it would be a measure that established itself on its own, as it were, through the interaction between claim and response, whereby "Being" and its claim would be what "provides the measures."

How does a measure emerge for the thinking of one who, eksisting, stands in the truth of Being? Heidegger provides us with no answer to this and other similar questions, neither in the "Letter on Humanism" nor in his later writings. We do not know exactly how we ought to think of this nonmetaphysical measure. The problem becomes even more urgent if one points out that in the "Letter on Humanism" Heidegger expressly refused to give "directives for our active life" (111, 236). There, he did defend the view that thinking is a "deed" that simultaneously "surpasses all praxis" (ibid., 115, 239; cf. 53,*193*ff.) and therefore "pervades" all action and production (ibid.). He also noted there the "obvious perplexity of man in our age" and asked, "Who could fail to see this distress?" (ibid., 104, 232); but he then restricted himself to the "sole matter of thinking," i.e., "to bring to language ever and again the advent of Being" (ibid., 118, 241). For him, this means determining "the truth of Being" and "the essence of man as ek-sistence" as a dwelling in this truth.

If, however, the measure for thinking and for poetry is supposed to be the measure for responsible action, the measure for the realm that the tradition has determined as "ethical," then it must be strongly emphasized that one of Heidegger's decisive insights is that Being "conceals" itself, that "withdrawal" reigns in various ways—as "mystery" and especially as the "errancy" that makes errors possible. What meaning should we attach to the essence of a nonmetaphysical measure that establishes itself in the relationship of claim and response as the "truth of Being," a relationship that essentially entails withdrawal, mystery, and errancy? Even if this can perhaps at best serve as a measure for poetry—a question that is not the subject of our investigation here—this is certainly not true of the meaning of a measure that is supposed to serve as a measure for responsible action. It cannot serve as the sense of that measure by virtue of which man, in his taking of measure, is able to make the distinction between good and evil, a measure without which man has no motive for preferring good to evil.

In his later writings, Heidegger thought of the "abode in the truth of Being" as "poetic dwelling" (*VA* 187ff., 219ff.), and this as dwelling in the "fourfold" (cf. ibid., 145ff., 150ff.). Our question will thus be whether or not and, if so, in which sense, the fourfold contains a measure for the "mortals" who dwell within it.

Here, however, I would like to interrupt this presentation in order to trace a certain development prior to the "Letter on Humanism." In this development, the constellation of issues that the tradition has determined as "ethics"—and therein determined as free moral decision—are absorbed and come to an end in the issue of truth (*alētheia*). It is interesting to trace this development since the absorption of the determination of "freedom" into that of "truth" also made it impossible to find a measure for responsible action—at least in the traditional sense of a measure.

Is the Determination of Truth, into Which Freedom Is Incorporated, a Measure for Responsible Action?

In *Being and Time,* the matter at issue in the determination "freedom" or "being free" and the one involved in the determination "truth" were still treated as distinct phenomena.[8] "Freedom" and "being-free" were expressions for the "resoluteness" of *Dasein* in its potentiality-for-Being, within the scope of its possibilities, in particular for the resoluteness of "authentic" *Dasein,* which is "guilty" in a sense different from the traditional one, and that wants to have "responsibility" as well as a "conscience" (288–89; cf. also *SK* 198, *164*). Furthermore, already in *Being and Time* an attempt was made to show that "*Dasein's* disclosedness attains the most primordial phenomenon of 'truth' insofar as *Dasein is* essentially its disclosedness" (221). "Authentic disclosedness" is said to be the phenomenon of the "most primordial truth in the mode of authenticity," "the truth of existence" (ibid.). Heidegger's identification of the concept of truth with that of freedom as disclosedness in *Being and Time,* as well as the attempt to exhibit truth as the uncoveredness of beings within the world, led Heidegger to the problems he took up in his subsequent writings, "What Is Metaphysics," "The Essence of Reasons," and, above all, "On the Essence of Truth." For the question of how the issues traditionally connected with the term "freedom" came to be less and less significant in Heidegger's thought, the latter lecture is of special importance. For there, not only are the traditional views of the essence of freedom replaced by another determination of its essence, but, furthermore, the everyday ways in which one takes measure become less important, and it is perhaps for just this reason that one loses a sense of the necessity for a measure that can serve as an ethical orientation.

In spite of its title, one gets the impression that this lecture is concerned with the essence of freedom rather than the essence of truth. It is stated that "the essence of truth unveils itself as freedom" (*WdW* 19, *130*). However, what kind of freedom is it that man possesses? The answer is, "Man does not 'possess' freedom as a property; rather, at best, the converse holds: freedom, the ek-sistent, disclosive *Da-sein* possesses man and does this so originally that *it* alone grants mankind that relationship to being as a whole and as such that founds and distinguishes all history" (17, *129*). Heidegger still defends this view in his commentary on Schelling, where he even expresses it in the form of a maxim: "Freedom is not a property of man; man is rather the property of freedom" (*SK* 11, *9*).[9] Compared with the analysis of *Dasein* in *Being and Time,* this is an even more basic renunciation of the "subjectivism" that had been fully realized in German idealism's determination of "subjectivity" as freedom. Just how far Heidegger in "On the Essence of Truth" deviated from this as well as from other traditional determinations of freedom is demonstrated by the fact that freedom was now determined as a "letting beings be" (cf. *WdW* 15, *127*). Heidegger understood this "letting be of beings" as adhering to something opened up as such, and by this he means "beings" (cf. ibid., 12, *125*); it is a way of becoming involved "in the open" and its openness (ibid., 15, *127*) into which every being comes to stand, bringing that openness, as it were, along with it. According to this early lecture, this openness, which was Heidegger's sole concern in this determination of the essence of freedom, is the *alētheia* that had been experienced by the early Greeks and that Heidegger had translated in *Being and Time* as "unconcealment" [*Unverborgenheit*] instead of as "truth" (16, *127*). There, the usual concept of truth in the sense of a correct statement was changed around in order to think it back to that which is still "uncomprehended in the disclosedness and disclosing of Being" (16, *128*). Becoming involved in this "disclosedness of beings" as a "letting be," i.e., freedom (cf. ibid.) is, as Heidegger declares, "prior to all of this ('negative' and 'positive' freedom); [freedom is] involvement in the disclosure of beings as such" (ibid.). Seen in this way, freedom is the "ek-sistence that is rooted in truth." It is the "exposition in the disclosedness of Being as such" (ibid. 17, *130*). This, however, is then understood as "beings as such and as a whole" (ibid.), which is then explicitly termed the "*Being* of beings" (ibid., 26, *139*) a few pages later. Here we shall not pursue how, already at this point, Heidegger's determination of "beings as such and as a

whole" connected Being with the development of "Western history"; and we cannot pursue the intimation that it is a "time" that
"itself immeasurable, first opens up that open realm for each measure" (ibid., 17, 129). It is important for us to realize that precisely
because "truth [is] in essence freedom," historical mankind can, in
the letting be of beings, also allow beings to *not* be the beings they
are and as they are; beings are then "covered up and distorted,"
semblance can come to reign, and in it "the non-essence [*Unwesen*]
of truth can come to the fore" (cf. ibid., 18, 130). Without any genuine explanation, this "untruth" is then said to belong essentially together with truth.

The way that they belong together is of fundamental significance
for our question concerning the possibility of a "measure." In seeking an answer, it is especially important to make it clear that already here the Being of beings in Heidegger's terminology of the
time, beings as such and as a whole, manifests itself as an attunement, as a whole that cannot be defined or grasped, a whole that
permeates everything, both as openness and especially as concealment. But what is this concealment in its essence? If one thinks of it
in terms of truth as disclosure, then it is "nondisclosure" (ibid., 21,
133). In concealment, Heidegger recognizes "the genuine untruth
that is most proper to the essence of truth." In terms of ek-sisting
Dasein's letting-be, it is "nothing less than the concealing of that
which is concealed as a whole, of beings as such" (ibid.). It is precisely this "concealing of that which is concealed as a whole" and
only this that Heidegger calls "mystery" (ibid.). That *Dasein* that
lets beings be "relates" [*verhält*] itself to this concealment—a relationship "that thereby conceals itself, letting a forgottenness of the
mystery take precedence and itself disappearing in the process"
(ibid., 22, 134). In this context, Heidegger himself spoke of the "essence of providing measures" and the "ground for taking measure."
Nonetheless, he no more attempted to determine the "essence" of
a measure, the measure as such, here than he did later (see below,
p. 49). There is no indication here that he thought of the essence of
a measure with traits different from the metaphysical ones outlined above. Heidegger further declares that man can become the
victim of "not allowing the concealment of that which is concealed

to reign"; he can forget the "mystery of *Dasein*" and abide by the "latest needs and aims," fulfilling them with his projects and plans; he can cling to what is "customary [*Gangbare*] and to his own devices [*Gemächte*]," and—to put it more generally—"by forgetting Being as a whole," take his "measures" from what is commonplace (cf. ibid., 23, *134*). "He insists on it," Heidegger writes, "and continually equips himself with new measures without considering either the ground for his taking measures or the essence of giving a measure. Though man proceeds to new measures and goals, he is constantly mistaken with regard to the essential genuineness of his measures. He mismeasures the more exclusively he takes himself, as subject, to be the measure for all beings."

It is especially important to see that already in Heidegger's earlier thinking, the relationship of ek-sistence to concealment as the mystery is not merely a contingent deviation [*Abfallen*], but rather is the way that *Dasein* obstinately clings to that which is customary, "in-sists" upon it, and that such "insistence" belongs to the essence of *Dasein* as a being that ek-sists and "takes measure" (ibid., 23, *135*). By turning to whatever happens to be as such and taking that as its normative standard, *Dasein* essentially turns away from the mystery. "The insistent turning away toward what is customary and the ek-sistent turning away from the mystery belong together. They are one and the same" (ibid.). "Man's flight away from the mystery toward that which is customary, onward from one current thing on to the next, passing by the mystery" is called "erring" (ibid.). With regard to our question concerning a measure that would provide a point of orientation, Heidegger's most important insights, in my view, are that "errancy" belongs to the inner constitution of *Dasein,* into which historical man is placed; that this is the latitude [*Spielraum*] for the "turn" mentioned above; and still more important, that the concealment of the self-concealing of beings as a whole reigns in the revelation of whatever particular beings emerge and that such forgottenness of concealment becomes errancy. Errancy, however, is the basis for errors, it is the "kingdom (dominion) of the history of those entanglements in which all sorts of erring are interwoven" (ibid.). Heidegger says that all these kinds of erring as ways of comporting oneself to beings as a whole can be traced back to one basic error, which he calls errancy (cf. ibid.). However, the fact that man is led astray also makes it possible "that man is capable of drawing up out of his ek-sistence—the possibility that, by experiencing errancy itself and not mistaking the mystery of *Dasein,* he does *not* let himself be led astray" (ibid., 25, *136*). This can develop into the "resolute openness [*Ent-schlosenheit*] toward the mystery" that is "underway into errancy as such," and thus leads one to pose the question concerning the essence of truth in a more primordial manner. The mystery thus leads one out of errancy to the "question in the sense of the one and only question, what beings as such are as a whole," what "the *Being* of beings" is (ibid., 26, *137*).

For Heidegger it is because of his "forgetting" the mystery that man takes his measures from what is customary, that he is mistaken with regard to the essential genuineness of his measures, and that the "insistent" reliance upon what is customary, i.e., "erring," continues to prevent one from taking one's measures from "essentially genuine" measures. However, Heidegger has not shown wherein the "essentially genuine" measures lie, nor has he differentiated "nonmetaphysically" conceived measures from those conceived of "metaphysically."

Looking back on the determinations in the "Letter on Humanism" of 1947 as discussed above, and considering the thoughts that had already been developed in "On the Essence of Truth," we are urgently confronted with the following question: Does evil as an essential form of malice perhaps also belong to the "concealing of that which is concealed," the mystery, or is it one of the ways of erring that arises from "errancy"? In either case, this means that the pivotal determination in the "Letter on Humanism," namely, "the truth of Being," would not be a "measure" for responsible action—regardless of whether the term "measure" is thought of "metaphysically" or "nonmetaphysically." Perhaps it would then hold that in a given case someone who, according to the general opinion, is acting in an evil manner could either appeal to the fact that the hale did not disclose itself out of the concealment of that which is concealed as a whole, that the mystery did not reveal itself. Or one could appeal to the fact that he had fallen victim to the errancy that belongs essentially to *Dasein*. It would not only be impossible to speak of "guilt" and "accountability" for his evil deed, or of his "responsibility"; even on the assumption that Heidegger founded his determinations on a nonmetaphysical conception of essence, one could not discern whether or not and to what extent the particular "assignments" [*Zuweisungen*] that are to be the "laws" and "rules" for those who have found their "abode in the truth of Being," are still permeated by the "mystery" and "errancy" that belong to truth.

Are *Gestell*[10] and Other Forms of the History of Being Measures for Responsible Action?

In the lecture "The Question Concerning Technology" (1953), Heidegger commented on the traditional concept of freedom once again and stated where the essence of freedom lay for him. "Freedom," he wrote, "is *originally* not connected with the will or even with the causality of human willing" (*VA* 24, *306*). A few sentences further we read: "The freedom of one who is free consists neither in unfettered arbitrariness, nor in his being bound by mere laws" (ibid., 25, *306*). This determination, polemically directed against traditional views of the essence of freedom, is justified only by an allusion to what Heidegger considers to be the original essential determination of freedom. On closer investigation, it turns out that this determination coincides with the determination of the essence of truth as developed in the "Letter of Humanism." Instead of speaking of the "truth of Being," however, Heidegger now speaks of the "occurrence of disclosing." "The occurrence of disclosing, i.e. of truth, is that to which freedom stands in the closest and most intimate kinship" (ibid., 24, *306*). "This freedom," he continues, "is that which conceals in a way that opens to light, in whose lighting shimmers that veil that enshrouds the essential occurrence of truth and allows the veil to appear as that which enshrouds" (ibid.). Our thesis that in Heidegger's thinking the traditional concept of "freedom" is absorbed in the concept of "truth" and that the latter is in turn absorbed in a determination that is quite different from the traditional one then holds for the later Heidegger as well.

Was there any change in Heidegger's position on the term "truth" subsequent to the 1930 essay "On the Essence of Truth"? Already in 1935 in the lecture "The Origin of the Work of Art" it was shown that the conception of truth as "correctness" is not "originary." The "essence" of truth was shown to be the occurrence of clearing that must be thought of in a verbal sense, as clearing that, at the same time, is in itself concealing, the "alternation" [*Gegenwendige*] of clearing and concealing. It is the "alternation" of mystery and dissembling (errancy) on the one hand, and disclosedness on the other. The further development of the concept of truth proceeded from the "equal value" of clearing and concealing, of *alētheia* and *lēthē*, but eventually led concealment to be determined as the "source" of clearing and finally as the "heart" of *alētheia* (cf. *ZSD* 78, *391*). That which is disclosed within disclosedness comes to remain permeated by mystery and dissembling.

This is one development. The other is that Heidegger increasingly came to think "in terms of the *Geschick* of Being" [*seinsgeschicklich*]. Being, for which it had turned out to be impossible to provide a foundation, showed itself to Heidegger as a *Geschick* in the form of various *Schickungen* to thought and poetry, as well as— as we just showed in our discussion of the "Letter on Humanism"—to mankind as such. Together, these single *Schickungen* constitute a nonteleologically ordered "history of Being," the *Geschick* of Being in general. This development is of great significance for our question of whether or not and if so, then how, there is a "measure" in Heidegger's thinking that is also binding for responsible action. For it could be that he considered "measure" to be that which comes to be in an essential way and, as a *Geschick* of Being, reigns in each particular "unconcealedness." Can one not, for instance, say that the essential unfolding of technology that reigns today as unconcealment, namely the *Gestell,* is a measure and is so even according to the traditional characteristics of a measure developed above? This assumption seems to be confirmed by Heidegger's explicit statement that man has no command over the particular unconcealedness reigning at a given time or over that which comes to occur essentially within it; it is no "human handiwork" (*TuK* 17–18, *299–300*). *Gestell* thus has a "transcendent" kind of Being that is absolutely valid in a particular epoch but that is at the same time "immanent" to those who live in that epoch. *Gestell,* Heidegger declares, determines man as he finds himself in this unconcealedness; the *Gestell* determines man in his "meditating and striving, shaping and working, entreating and thanking" (ibid. 18, 300). It has the power to permeate one who listens to it to an extent such that, with no further reflection whatsoever, he must follow it as something obligatory and binding. Whoever is set upon by the *Gestell* "responds" to it in his labor by disclosing beings whose kind of Being is that of *Bestand.*[11] *Gestell,* in unfolding its essence in this manner, thus also has the traits of being manifest and univocal.

Now it is part of all epochs of the *Seinsgeschick*—with the exception of that *Geschick* that was sent to the thinking of the Presocratics—that they are "epochs of errancy." Each and every one of them belongs completely to the *Seinsgeschick* called metaphysics; they are all ways in which the creative sense of Being experienced by the Presocratics withdraws. They are suspensions of the creative sense of Being and hence epochs of the "errancy" that belongs to the "essential unfolding of truth," as Heidegger showed at an early stage. As such, they represent a "necessary" danger—necessary because "man misconstrues the unconcealed and misinterprets it" (ibid., 26, 307). The reign of the *Geschick* sent in the form of *Gestell* is the "supreme danger" because here this misinterpretation is most extreme. Just as in "On the Essence of Truth" it takes "false" measures as its reference. Being, reigning as the *Geschick* sent in errancy, is what now leads man astray in his measure-taking.

Even if that which essentially emerges in each particular unconcealedness seems to exhibit the traditional traits of a measure, because of this "necessary danger" that leads man astray, it therefore cannot be conceived of as a measure. The only thing that could be such a measure would be the "more primal truth" (ibid., 28, 309) for thinking that sets out preparatively to project an "other" beginning in human experience. What it projects is the "world" in the form of the "fourfold" [*Geviert*]. We shall therefore address ourselves to Heidegger's later work with the question of whether the essence of Being that in such anticipatory thinking takes on the form of world, has the character of a measure that could provide man with a point of orientation in his efforts to distinguish between good and evil and find a motivation for preferring good to evil.

Is the Fourfold a Measure for Responsible Action?

In *Schelling's Treatise on the Essence of Human Freedom,* Heidegger determined Being as "an arrangement of jointures [*Gefüge*]." In his later writings, he conceived of this determination as the unity of an arrangement of jointures that is made up of four realms, as the fourfold.

Since we have until now received a negative answer to our question whether the determinations "truth of Being" and "dwelling in the truth of Being" can be understood as "measures," we shall inquire into whether the "contentual determinations" of "the truth of Being," i.e., the worlding world thought in anticipatory thinking and the mirror-play of the fourfold, can lead to an affirmative answer.[12]

As far as the structure of the fourfold, the "fouring" itself is concerned, the answer to the question must be negative because of the mere fact that it possesses an *alētheia*-structure, a relatedness as unconcealedness, both with regard to the whole of the fouring as well as with regard to the relationship of the four regions to each other. This relatedness realizes itself in the fourfold as its inner mobility. Heidegger thought of it as a "playing" and as a "mirror." The concealment that remains present in unconcealment, the mystery, and the four regions that play together with and mirror one another lead to an ambiguity; and this ambiguity stands in contradiction to an important trait of a measure taken in the traditional sense, namely its univocal character. Furthermore, the basic instability inherent in playing and mirroring is irreconcilable with the traditional meaning of a measure.

Is there not, however, one region, that of the divinities, that could serve as a measure for orienting oneself in responsible action? Heidegger explicitly declares that mortals "are awaiting intimations of their [i.e., the divinities'] coming" (*VA* 151, 328).

This chapter began with the assumption that the region of the "divine," of the "heavenly beings," was the region that provided measures for both Hölderlin and Schelling. It is, however, inconceivable that Heidegger—for whom there was no longer an "absolute" God and for whom the idea of man as created in his image and likeness was without force, and who sought to surmount the "onto-theological constitution of metaphysics"—should have reverted to a strictly "theological" position.

According to Heidegger's determination of God, God appears as what he is in the "concealed sway" of the divinities (*VA* 177, *178*). In the lecture ". . . Poetically Man Dwells . . ." this appearance is nevertheless determined such that it is not a genuine "revelation." God, as he who remains unknown, is "manifest only in the heavens" (197, *222*) and the heavens are said not to be "sheer light" (ibid., 201, *226*). That God who "remains unknown," who is manifest only in the heavens, is a "measure"—though this measure holds only for the way the poet derives his measures, i.e., for one who "safeguards that which is concealed in its concealing" (cf. below, p. 155). Can a God who remains so concealed be a true measure for man in his search for orientation for responsible action (such as divine love was for Schelling)?

A measure taken in the traditional sense has the traits of manifestness and thus univocality. This is the only way that a measure had binding force. But could one not say of the "divinities" that they and their intimations provide a measure for mortals? The divinities are one of the four regions within the mirror-play. As we have seen, the mirror-play has an *alētheia*-structure. This implies that each region is unconcealed, that its essence is therefore also determined by concealment, the mystery. Furthermore, the region of the "divinities" stands, as does each of the other regions within the fouring, in relation to the other three; and they for their part also have the structure of *alētheia* and are unconcealed only out of the concealment that is also present in them. Moreover, the mirroring into the other three regions constitutes part of the content involved in the determination of the "divinities." The mortals, the earth, and the heavens play into the unconcealedness of the divinities such that this unconcealedness not only bears the sense of the divine, but bears at the same time the sense of the mortal, the earth, and the sky. The region of the divinities in this ambiguous form cannot be a measure for mortals, even though they wait expectantly for the divinities as such; it cannot serve as a measure for an orientation that would let the difference between the "hale" and "malice" come forth, nor can it give mortals a motivation for preferring the hale to malice; and the same is true of the intimations that mortals are awaiting.

In the "Letter on Humanism," Heidegger had spoken of the "dimension of the holy" (102, *252;* 86ff., *218ff.*). As such, would this not be a measure that could serve as a point of orientation for responsible action? Even though this dimension is not one of the "regions" within the fouring, which, as we have shown, are opposed to the traditional understanding of a measure, nevertheless it still resembles them insofar as Heidegger declares that it is precisely this dimension that can remain "closed off" to us. Indeed, the fact that the dimension of the holy is closed to us is, in Heidegger's view, "what distinguishes this age of the world" (ibid.). Thus the holy, according to the determination by which Heidegger conceived of it, cannot provide a measure for responsible action.

Can this be said of the region of the mortals by itself, that men as mortals "bear within themselves their measure," that in consonance with their essential determination of "being capable of death as death" (*VA* 196, *222*) mortals have an "inner hold," a stability within them that makes it possible for them simply to do what should be done and to avoid what one should not do—in a sense similar to Aristotle's *phronēsis* that provides one with the *noēsis,* the intuitive and reliable insight into the mean between two extremes with regard to the way one must act in the right place and at the right time? But even if Heidegger had considered this possibility of an "inner" measure, the question would still remain: By what means does one determine that that which one immediately intuits is "what should be done," and wherein does this distinguish itself from what one should refrain from doing? Wherein lies the motivation for the agent to prefer what one should do over that which one should not, i.e., good as opposed to evil?

Does not the determination of the fourfold and its regions perhaps contain another, *nonmetaphysically* conceived measure for responsible action that Heidegger himself did not develop as such? The view that it might contain such a nonmetaphysical measure seems plausible if one recalls the further determination of the four-ing at the end of the lecture "The Thing": the fouring, as this "worlding of the world," as a mirror-play, is said to be a "round dance of appropriating" [*Reigen des Ereignens*]. "The round dance is the ring that joins in its play as mirroring" (*VA* 179, *180*). The four regions, these four primordial ways of human Being—the earth, the heavens, mortals, and the divinities—play in a "joining mirror-play of the world" [*ringendem Spiegel-Spiel der Welt*]. Is the "gathered presence" [*gesammeltes Wesen*] of this playing, the "ringing" [*Gering*], a nonmetaphysical measure? Such a measure would not confront man as a normative standard but would rather constitute itself in a "step back" (ibid., 180, *181*) into conduct that would "respond" to this playing.

We faced the same question in our consideration of the "truth of Being," although we did not pursue the determination of its contents. There, however, we came to a negative conclusion because, for Heidegger, mystery and above all errancy belong to the determination of truth. Here in the determination of the fourfold, there is no longer any mention of errancy; but mystery is indeed mentioned, as we have seen. It could be that the character of mystery is reconcilable with the essence of measure when the latter is conceived of nonmetaphysically whereas it is not when measure is conceived of traditionally, i.e., metaphysically. However, this certainly does not hold for the measure that we are seeking, i.e., for a measure for responsible action. It should, by the way, also be noted that Heidegger came to expound on the mirror-play of the fourfold, the "ringing," only with reference to the way the world emerges in the "thinging of the thing." Thus, subsequent to the determination of the world as "ringing," it is stated that the "thinging of the thing comes into its own [*ereignet sich*] out of the mirror-play of ringing in its joining" (ibid., 179, *180*). According to Heidegger, the surmounting of the currently reigning *Seinsgeschick,* i.e., *Gestell,* will occur from within that way in which a thing essentially comes to be. Only after the "fourfold" as "truth" has become part of the thing, has thus freed it from its "injurious neglect" (*TuK* 40–44, *41–47*) and thereby also from the "presumption of all unconditionedness" (*VA* 179, *47*) does this surmounting occur.

The issue in the determination of a measure in the Hölderlin

Erläuterung ". . . Poetically Man Dwells . . ." (cf. below, pp. 147–57)
is not a measure for orientation with regard to responsible action,
but rather the measure that the poet takes "for the construction of
[poetic] dwelling" (*VA* 202, 227), even though for Heidegger this is
also the measure that as such "measures out the essence of man." In
another chapter we shall examine the way that Heidegger made
use of the verse "poetically man dwells" from the poem "In Lovely
Blueness" as well as other texts in order to determine what Hölderlin meant by "man's measure." At this point, however, it is important to note only that Heidegger did not at all alter Hölderlin's basic
conviction from which we proceeded at the outset of this study:
man's measure, in light of which man measures himself, is God, and
"on earth" there is for man "no measure." The fact that Heidegger
ever determines measure to be the "appearance" of the unknown
God as one who is unknown through the openness of the heavens
and in the end takes "the heavens as the measure" (ibid., 201, 222),
the fact that in his view there is no measure on earth for Hölderlin
because man does not let "the earth be as earth in his dwelling"—
all this serves to indicate that he tried to integrate the regions of the
fourfold into his commentary. However, of the regions of the fourfold, the relationship of mortals to death is dealt with only peripherally in Heidegger's repeated maxim that they are "capable of death
as death." Yet it is precisely man's relationship to death, the experience of his mortality, that, if thought further, could provide a measure for orientation for responsible action. The primary intention
of this study is to demonstrate just this point. In order to do so, we
shall therefore complete the transition into the nonmetaphysical
dimension opened up by Heidegger and, following an examination
of his determination of the experience of death, I shall propose my
own conception of such a measure.

3. The Conception of a Nonmetaphysical Ethics Concerned
with One's Fellow Man

The theme of the following reflections is the determination of
death from the point of view of man's experience of himself as a
mortal. The issue is not death taken as the opposite of "life," as that
which nonbelievers consider to be nothing.

Does Heidegger's Determination of the Experience of Death Contain a Measure Thought of in an "Other" Way?

The later Heidegger does not conceive of death as bodily decay[13] or as a unique event that occurs at the end of one's life. Rather, he considers it a "power" that determines us throughout our lives such that we are constantly "dying." We can experience our being mortal if we are knowingly "capable of death as death" [*den Tod als Tod vermögen*][14] and have "become mortals" (cf. *VA* 177, *178,* and below, pp. 99–117). In the lecture "The Thing," Heidegger determined death as the "shrine of Nothing" (ibid.) and at another point as the "supreme shelter [*Gebirg*] of the mystery of disclosure in its calling" (256, *101*), as the "supreme concealment of Being" (*UzS* 23, *200*), the most profound mystery, but also as that which, because of its *alethēia*-structure, simultaneously calls into "disclosure" (cf. below, pp. 106–10).

Our first question is the following: If we proceed from the determination of a traditional, metaphysical measure that was developed above, then can death in this Heideggerian sense be considered a measure that would provide us with orientation? We can immediately rule out this possibility since death as the "supreme concealment of Being" is by no means consonant with the traditional essential traits of a measure's being manifest and univocal.

We may then inquire into whether Heidegger's determination of death contains any indication that he thought of it as a nonmetaphysical essence of measure. In posing the question in this manner, we are purposely entering into the element of an "other thinking": we are leaving behind traditional methods of deduction and dialectical presentation, of founding things in foundationalist contexts, and we are placing our reliance on experience, in particular on the experience of "attunements" [*Gestimmtheit*] as a legitimate access to "truth," a kind of truth, however, that is not identical with the truth of judgments.

I have already briefly described how Heidegger made use of poetic experience in the essay ". . . Poetically Man Dwells . . ." to determine the heavens as the measure for the poet, the heavens that are "not sheer light" and in which the "unknown God" appears as He who is unknown. At a later point we shall examine this point more closely; what is interesting here, however, is that Heidegger himself called this measure a "strange measure" (198, 223) and referred to the way the poet takes his measure as a "distinctive kind of measuring" (ibid., 199, 224), since this "measuring" is a "guarding of that which is concealed in its self-concealing" (ibid., 197, 223). This measure would be "nonmetaphysical." Cannot death in its extension into mortal existence [*Dasein*] also be seen as Heidegger's attempt to conceive of a nonmetaphysical measure? Measuring would then be the explicit experience of being mortal; it would be the way that mortals are "capable of death as death." At first glance, there seems to be no evidence in Heidegger's later writings for such a view. However, one should recall that death is not only the "supreme concealment of Being," but also its "supreme shelter," its "calling disclosure." Does this not imply that it grants openness, unconcealedness? That is precisely what I intend to show in a later chapter (cf. below, pp. 99–117). Furthermore, there is a passage in the lecture *Der Satz vom Grund* in which Heidegger determines death as that which, "being *Dasein*'s most extreme possibility, is capable of the utmost in the clearing of Being and its truth" (186–87).

If death is the "utmost clearing," then could it not set standards insofar as it grants a measure that is other than those conceived of in the tradition? The determination just quoted is in fact followed by the statement, "Death is the still unthought giving of a measure by that which is immeasurable, i.e., by the utmost play into which earthbound man is engaged, a play in which he is at stake" (ibid.).

According to the quotation, what is "immeasurable" for death's measure-giving is Being thought of as play. In a later essay in this volume, I will show how death is a "third force" over against Being and nihilating Nothing; as such, in positing the difference between the two and in its ability to separate them as distinct from one another, death "gives a measure." In doing so, however, I am consciously setting myself in opposition to Heidegger's fundamental conviction that Being is "nihilating," that "nihilating nothingness essentially unfolds in Being" (*HB* 113–14, 238–39). The fact that death "is capable of the utmost in the clearing of Being and its truth" shows that Being is indeed distinct from nihilating Nothing. As the "utmost" in the clearing of the truth of Being, it must resemble its "content," Being, in being completely free from any kind of nihilating Nothing. We shall return to this point both later in this chapter and in a subsequent chapter.

Our question concerning the possibility of a measure for orientation in one's responsible action is not concerned with the relationship of death to Being taken as play, but rather with the relationship of mortals to their death, which reaches into their existence and therefore can be experienced by them as such.

Within the nonmetaphysical dimension he opened, Heidegger did not think of death as a measure and he did not redetermine the essential traits of a measure.

The Essential Ontological Character of Attunement in Heidegger's Thinking: Anxiety

The issue we shall take as the point of departure for our conception of a nonmetaphysical ethics concerned with one's fellow man will be man's attunement [*Gestimmtheit*] in his relationship to death. In defining this relationship in the lectures "The Thing" and "Building, Dwelling, Thinking," Heidegger paid no attention to the attunement underlying it. This is noteworthy, for it is recognized that one of *Being and Time*'s foremost achievements is its phenomenological demonstration of the "essential ontological character of state-of-mind [*Befindlichkeit*]"[15] (cf. 135ff., 184ff., 342ff., 383). Moods were thought of there as the "originary way of Being in which *Dasein* is disclosed to itself prior to all knowing and willing, beyond their range of disclosure." It was shown how it is anxiety that, as a "fundamental state-of-mind, existentially constitutes *Dasein*'s openness to the world." It "confronts [*Dasein*] with its ownmost thrownness" and thereby unveils the uncanniness of everyday, familiar Being-in-the-world in order to raise "authentic" *Dasein* from Being-in-the-world as thrownness to Being-toward-death (ibid., 344). It is on the basis of "disclosedness" as an existentiale of *Dasein* that this occurs: in the "mood of resoluteness," which "is a moment of vision [*augenblicklich*], *Dasein* looks at those situations which are possible in its potentiality-for-Being-a-whole as disclosed in our anticipation of death" (ibid., 345).

In the inaugural lecture "What Is Metaphysics?" the phenomenological analysis turns into a speculative one. The fundamental

state-of-mind of anxiety is determined with the intention of making visible *Dasein's* relation to Nothing and, in particular, to the way
that Nothing permeates Being in a "nihilating" manner. As a result
of Heidegger's analysis, this "Being" does not show itself as something that is known logically by a self-knowing Being. It is experienced in the specific attunement of a "self" that has freed itself
from everything that has to do with objects and has also experienced itself as "finite."[16] Even after the "turn," Heidegger still
seems to have seen the importance of the "essential ontological
character" of attunement. However, attunement is thought of there
as a "corresponding" answer to a "claim" placed on man. Thus, we
read in the Addendum to "What Is Metaphysics?" written in 1943:
"The readiness for anxiety is the earnestness of the 'yes' to fulfill
the highest claim that alone touches man's essence. Of all beings,
man alone, by being called upon by the voice of Being, experiences
the wonder of all wonders: *that* being *is.*"

The question is whether or not this characterization of attunement as "essential anxiety" is appropriate after the "turn". *Being
and Time* showed that anxiety in the face of death is concerned
about Being-in-the-world as such. For those who have become
"mortals," those who have seen with open eyes that they are constantly dying and how they are doing so, the efficacy of death is
what induces an attunement that corresponds to this occurrence.
Heidegger did not thematize the attunement of mortals—which,
in our analysis, should by no means be misinterpreted as something psychological. It must instead be understood as something
that reveals and conceals Being and is in this sense "ontological."
We should recall, however, that those who have become mortals
are those who experience that their essential ways of sustaining
and producing life are continually unsettled. If they do not close
their eyes to this fact, then they must admit that they are always on
the way to ruin, to "calamity" [*Unheil*]. They not only experience
the workings of "nihilating Nothing" as something "that is different
from all being" (*WiM* 45); they also experience it as something
other than the occurrence of Being that gives them life and meaning. Faced with the efficacy of death within their *Dasein,* they experience how death, as a third force, distinguishes between nihilating
Nothing and Being and separates them from one another.

The Attunement of Unsettling Dread and
the Conversion into the Healing Force Within It

In the view expressed here, where does the efficacy of death's
extension into mortals' existence lie? Death unsettles, dis-places
mortals from their accustomed habits and relationships with
things. Above all, however, it wrests them from their everyday
way of "Being-with-others." The unsettling character of death can
be seen especially in the fact that it thrusts man back upon himself
as one who must bear death without the help of others as long as
he lives. The attunement that corresponds to this unsettling [*ent-
setzende*] power of death is that of veritable "dread" [*Ent-setzen*],
horror, or even desperation.

Sometimes death's unsettling effect on man lasts only a short
while. At the same time, however, it and its attendant attunement
can—like a jolt—"set one on a path" whose result is exactly the
opposite of unsettling dread and its attunement.

How is one to conceive of this "being set on a path" by dread?
Where does it occur? Does it take place on the "ontological" level
or within the realm of one's attunement? Let us briefly recall Heidegger's position. In *Being and Time,* for example, the description of the
way that the burden of *Dasein* is suddenly turned into the relief that
leads to an attunement of hope was given in an analysis of *Dasein*
within the realm of its attunement. By contrast, in the "Addendum" to "What Is Metaphysics?" cited earlier, the "path" from the
attunement of anxiety that touches one's very essence [*wesenhafte
Angst*] to the attunement that makes it possible to experience the
"wonder of all wonders" and becomes "awe" (47, 355) is first demonstrated on the level of Being. It is said to be the claim of Being, its
"voice" (ibid., 47, 354) [*Stimme*], that dispatches man into an "attuning" [*Stimmen*]. This attuning "claims man in his essence, so that
man learns to experience Being in Nothing" (ibid., 46, 354–55). It is
precisely here that one important aspect of the "turn" in Heidegger's
thought may be found, an aspect he tried to demonstrate "ontologically" in a number of ways (cf. below, p. 103). However, it must
be emphasized that in the passage cited, Heidegger still thought of
the "turn" as a reversal within the realm of attunement just as, in

Being and Time, he had thought of the turn as one from anxiety into awe. However, attunement here has the character of a "corresponding": it corresponds to the occurrence of Being, but this "reversal" still takes place solely within the realm of attunement. In a very similar manner, we shall conceive of the occurrence of unsettling dread brought about by death's extension into mortals' existence in an ontological way, whereby the reversal takes place within the realm of the attunement that accompanies this occurrence, and is thus itself "ontological."

In Heidegger's earlier view, the attunement of anxiety sets *Dasein* on the the way to authenticity, which subsequently establishes itself as the freedom unto death. After the "turn," the attunement of anxiety, which reaches into one's very essence, attunes one's thought so that one's conduct becomes a "guardianship of Being."

For us, the attunement that corresponds to the unsettling occurrence is the veritable dread that can develop into various degrees of horror up to complete desperation. Nonetheless, the "result" of reversal, the path within the realm of one's attunement, can be that man attains an attunement that overcomes dread and is in this sense a "healing force." This is our thesis. Is it not, however, a highly unrealistic view? Is it not overly optimistic? How can such a view be "founded?"

We must once again remind ourselves that, within the realm of nonmetaphysical thinking we have entered, there can be no "founding" in the metaphysical sense. We cannot attempt to prove the "necessity" of this path. We can only show that it is possible. But is it really possible? Is it a path upon which those who "have become mortals" could and would embark? At this point, we must first recall what Heidegger held to be man's current understanding of himself in the "epoch of errancy" predominant today. This understanding is still that man is an *animal rationale,* a living being whose pathway is determined by *ratio.* According to the determinations Heidegger developed in his preparatory thinking, human beings must first "become" mortals if they are to "dwell" poetically in the "world" within a dwelling, whose measures are taken from the poet in his architectonics—a dwelling that must be preceded by a fundamental transformation in man with regard to his "Being-with" others. Heidegger did not tell us anything about the process

of this transformation. However, I am convinced that human intersubjectivity could be changed from one in which the other's form
of Being-for-us is such that he is "merely present-at-hand" into one
where there is a "Being-together-with-one-another." The task is,
then, to show the steps involved in this development. In this path
of experience, I see the foundation for a nonmetaphysical ethics
that Heidegger himself did not think through. In tracing out this
development, we are proceeding from the assumption mentioned
earlier in the Introduction, the assumption that only the *possibility*
of such a path can be demonstrated; but even if most people avoid
facing this possibility, it is nevertheless one that represents the
"truth" of human Being and can thus serve as the foundation for a
nonmetaphysical ethics concerned with one's fellow man. The
"matter itself" [*Sache selbst*], being mortal, is evident not only to
those who philosophize but also to anyone who has escaped from
the forces that lead to the everyday concealment of this "truth."
Who would deny that we are "constantly dying" in the sense characterized above and that all can hence have this experience if,
through ever-renewed efforts to have this experience, they do not
deny its truth to themselves? Our demand both that these efforts
be made and that an indifferent Being-with-others must be overcome also has its justification in the matter at issue. And it is precisely this issue that we want to try to render explicit by employing a suitable method, namely the phenomenological method.

A Phenomenological Description of the Pathway from the
Unsettling to the Healing Force

I shall attempt a phenomenological description of how death, in its
extension into *Dasein,* turns into the experience of mortality. I shall
describe how it can thereby unfold itself as the experience of a
"healing power" in whose forms there can be the "other" measure
for responsible action we have been seeking.

    In a moment of "sudden insight," the meaning of the statement
"I am constantly dying" becomes clear. It is this "intuition" that has
such an immediately "unsettling" effect: it wrests man from his
previous state of Being and its corresponding attunement.

    Hitherto, even if only in a vague way, one was conscious of oneself as a being that lived in complete indifference to its mortality, in a sort of certainty that one had an almost "eternal subsistence." At the same time, one was conscious of one's "Being-with" others, was aware of them in diverse forms of interaction; but one encountered them in the mode of Being "co-present-at-hand" like "things," things that have the significance of something ready-to-hand [*zuhandene*] or present-at-hand [*vorhandene*], as Heidegger has shown in *Being and Time* in his analysis of the worldhood of *Dasein's* environment in the mode of everydayness. What is decisive is that man's relationship to himself and to others had been confined to the attunement of total indifference.

This sudden insight unsettles, displaces one from this state of Being and attunement. This insight unmasks them as "mere appearances" [*Schein*], and compels me to look my "mortality" as the "truth" of my Being in the face. The question is, how does the attunement of indifference become transformed into that of unsettling dread, and how is it that through this the "truth" of my Being emerges more poignantly?

First of all, I become aware in a more radical way that death, which extends into my very Being [*Dasein*], continually undermines, subverts my efforts to produce, sustain, and promote life, only to thwart them completely in the end. I experience myself as being on the way to certain "disaster" [*Unheil*]; and, above all, I experience myself as thrust back upon myself alone. I must face this impending disaster all by myself. The shock trembling through me dissolves my consciousness into utter helplessness. This is the attunement that has now replaced indifference and has shown that my previous state of being was a mere facade. My awareness of myself as isolated in utter helplessness is then the element through which my indifference to others as beings that are merely present-at-hand disappears. This is the element within which the indifference is gradually but increasingly transformed into a relationship to others that allows them to become my "fellow men." First, as a result of my having experienced that utter distress, they emerge as those to whom I turn, almost begging for help. And for just this reason they are no longer a matter of indifference to me. They have become those who can help me, helpers in my hour of need. Thus, a "path" has opened up that can make possible a transformation of my Being and the attunement that underlies it. This beginning tends toward a gradual development that is, however, by no means a "necessary" one. Often, perhaps even in most cases, one relapses into the old manner of relating to oneself and Being-with-others in which indifference predominates. The transformation was not profound enough. In other cases, however, human beings "become mortals."

Now that I have been thrust back upon myself and am alone, the experience of my isolation leads me to relate to others, to those who have left me all alone. Ever more clearly they show themselves to me as beings who—though they themselves are usually unaware of the fact—are subject to the same fate of being mortal, so that those whose help I seek are just as much in need of help themselves. They are also mortals delivered unto the unsettling force of dread. This means that they are no longer strangers but are rather "comrades" in the sense of those who share my fate and who in turn need me as a comrade. Moreover, it means that they even have a right to expect that I accept responsibility for them and that I intend to act responsibly—something we have assumed in this chapter, whose concern is not whether the other as such calls me to be responsible.[17] My slowly awakening and constantly increasing attunement is now one of solidarity; this solidarity has in turn a tendency to unfold itself further, and this unfolding also takes place in my being attuned. What were previously neutral and indifferent modes of "interaction" and "communication" become increasingly fraught with emotion. I feel increasingly that these comrades are friends and assume a similar development on their part, as I feel that I am accepted by them as a friend with the same inclinations. Thus, the form of intersubjectivity that is thoroughly in accord with indifference may gradually give way to a thou-community of friends who accept responsibility for each other, a relationship in which each person stands for the other and puts himself in the other's place.

When faced by the sheer force of death, dread dissolves everything that is static and leads one to the growing conviction that a calculating will is not capable of attaining everything for which it aims. This conviction could induce one to relinquish any attempt to have one's own way, so that a less coersive relationship would come about in which it would be a matter of course to accept a loving, kind, and just responsibility for others.

The way that this could result in "social consciousness" and its political institutions cannot be dealt with here. In any case, the constitution of such sociality would not require a commonly shared space as does a people who constitute a nation; and yet neither would it constitute itself abstractly as the community of "mankind."

The path upon which unsettling, dreadful death sends man can thus have the further result that man is healed by this attunement of unsettling dread. Someone who is healthy is only truly aware of himself *as* healthy when he experiences himself as no longer ill, and in this sense as "having been healed," so that he is now aware of himself as experiencing the state of health as a state of "being healed." Similarly, he who experiences himself as a "thou" within a community of "thous" could experience this community as "healing" [*heilende*] or, to use an antiquated term, as "hale" [*heil*]. The terms "healing" [*heilend*] and "healing force" [*das Heilende*] are used with the conscious exclusion of all other connotations associated with these terms. They refer to those mortals who live in the "truth of Being" concerning themselves and their fellow man, who dwell hale within the healing force. However, they "dwell" there only if this dwelling is not a temporary attunement but has rather taken on a concrete form, only if the change that has occurred in them has been established in lasting character traits and thereby come to be stabilized. The healing force can thus have taken on a form that resembles what the tradition has called love, compassion, and recognition of others, for instance. These forms of the healing power, then, would have become *measures* for one who intends to act responsibly, measures that underlie his whole Being and therefore do not confront him as demands or duties. Such a person would have already traversed the pathway that has led him to the attunement of a fraternal "thou."

The Nonmetaphysical Measure of the Healing Force
in Its Various Forms as a Way to Overcome
Transcendent Normative Standards

We recall that in *Being and Time* Heidegger determined the phenomenon of "hope" as an alleviation from the burden of *Dasein*. He
showed this in light of *Dasein's* relationship to "the thrown ground
of its Self" (345), a relationship that is a "path" within *Dasein's* ontological attunement. Our conception of the path from the attuned
experience of death to the attuned experience of the healing power
is analogous. Of course, after the turn, the path opened by the jolt
that issued from unsettling dread can no longer be derived from an
analysis of *Dasein* like the one in *Being and Time* where hope was
phenomenologically derived from the way that *Dasein* has always
previously "attained itself." The path that opens up within the attunement of human being that ek-sists in Being and that leads to
the healing force must be thought of as a "donation" [*Gabe*] to mortals. The fact that the path opens up and that one is led from the
attunement of calamity to that of the healing force must furthermore be thought of as an "event" [*Geschehen*] in the sense of something that happens to *Dasein*; and the "result" of this path, the healing force, must be thought of as a donation to mortals' experience,
as a "gift."

What does the experience of the healing force entail? First of all,
whoever experiences it must be able to accept this gift, for the experience of the healing force can have a healing effect only if it is
taken as something that has been bestowed as a gift. Furthermore,
this "sphere," this "realm," which within itself cannot be given a
foundation, is a source of giving and bestowing, a bestowing power
that is similar to a *causa sui*, an absolute. But how does this absolute, unfathomable power of the healing force perform its giving
and bestowing? The answer is that the healing force bestows by
acting as a measure. It bestows by establishing itself, by providing
its own support. Love, compassion, and recognition of others are
examples of the forms into which the healing force develops because, after a person has been completely changed, this healing
force—precisely in order to be able to heal—tends to change his

entire conduct. This is how the healing force differs from anxiety.
Can we grasp more precisely what it is that the healing force attains in these various forms?

Heidegger reached the nonmetaphysical dimension with the
help of the determinant "it gives" [*es gibt*], but he thinks of it as
an "appropriative event" [*Ereignis*],[18] as the appropriative event
thought of in a verbal sense. Moreover, he also incorporated Being
as thought of metaphysically into this event of appropriation (cf.
UzS 260, *129*). "Appropriating" as the "event of appropriation" refers to that which grants and safeguards each thing in the ownness
proper to it. These determinants are intended as a nonmetaphysical, "prepredicative" way of characterizing whatever *is* an event.
The determination "nearness" is first and foremost in this effort. In
his analysis of *Dasein*, Heidegger, through a determination of the
"Being-in" of those beings within the world that *Dasein* encounters,
had already thematized their "essential tendency to nearness"
(ibid., 105, *139–40*) and had pointed out the distinct sort of "nearness" and "distancing that belongs to concernful *Dasein*." Similarly,
in the later Heidegger one also finds that the determination "nearness" has a "spatial" aspect (cf. *UzS* 211ff., *104ff.*). This aspect continued to be a guiding force in his attempt to utilize "more original
thinking" in order to conceive of this "nearness" as "nearing" and
the latter as a "setting the regions of the world on the way toward
one another." His intention was to preclude space and time's having
"the character of parameters," which has led to the truthless neglect of the thing. Only when he was concerned with determining
the relationship between poetry and thinking as a "neighborhood"
did Heidegger remind us that it also is based on "nearness." Since in
Heidegger's view thinking and poetry are both extraordinary ways
of ek-sisting within Being, one can assert that he did not make use
of the determinations "nearness" and its "nearing" in order to characterize the way we conduct ourselves toward our fellow man.

However, does not the nearing nearness refer to the very "it
gives" that we are concerned with here, to the realm of "human
fellowship" that Heidegger had determined as an "existentiale of
Being-with-others" in *Being and Time*? Is not the nearness that
brings human beings closer to each other the same thing we attempted to conceive of as the reign of the healing force? Is it not the

same as that which, in a corresponding attunement, proved to be the outcome of the mortal's path that began with unsettling dread in the face of the experience of death? Does nearness not show itself precisely as that force that sets us on our way [*das Be-wëgende*] in the forms of the healing force that we know as love, compassion, and mutual human recognition?

Has our reference to Heidegger's determinations, in particular to "nearness," helped us make progress in our attempt to answer the question of where the essence of a nonmetaphysical measure lies as opposed to a metaphysical one? We have made progress only to the extent that we are now certain that we find ourselves on a level of a nonmetaphysical dimension where the issue concerns the realm of one's fellow man. This is the realm in which we can seek an answer to our question concerning a measure for responsible conduct. Can we recognize the essential determinations for an "other" essence of measure here?

It seems that those who engage in philosophy today between "the tradition and an other beginning" must first orient themselves with regard to the essential traits of a measure in the traditional sense developed above. But is the measure we have just unfolded still a normative standard, i.e., one that overrides any particular measure-taking and thus has "transcendence" as its kind of Being, but yet determines the one who takes a measure and therefore also has "immanence" as its kind of Being? The answer to this question is no. The kind of Being of the measure unfolded here is no longer the sort that takes measures from an objective normative standard that confronts man. On the contrary, he who takes measure "dwells" in the measure, it embraces him and determines him from the outset so that the kind of Being it takes on involves no merely subsequent "immanence." However, it does indeed appear that the traditional traits of a measure are still valid here. The healing force and its measures are, as measures, "absolute." For one who loves, who is compassionate and is capable of recognizing others, the other is unconditionally and immediately someone who is beloved, who arouses his compassion, to whom he grants recognition. The decisive characteristic of this nonmetaphysically conceived measure lies in its absoluteness, in the fact that it no longer has "transcendence" and "immanence" as its forms of Being, in its power to bind all in each and every case, in its obligatory character. Herein lies its obligation; and the essential trait of self-sameness lies in the fact that this obligation binds the one who loves, is compassionate, and grants others recognition, in each and every situation. For one who "dwells" in these measures, they are immediately evident. A measure thought of in this manner thus has the further essential traits of being manifest and univocal.

That a measure be absolute, obligatory, self-same, manifest, and univocal is the minimal requirement for whatever is to be associated with the colloquial sense of a measure today. We have also given a name to that which, in the traditional conception of measure, grants these traits: we have called it a "power" [Kraft]. Is it not also a "power" that is the basis for the nonmetaphysical determination of the "nearing nearness" such that this nearness is what exhibits itself as that which heals?

What does the term "power" mean here? It would be a relapse into metaphysics if we were to attempt to discover it "behind" the measure and the healing force as a principle that determines the totality of beings. Schelling, for instance, thought of such a power as the "world soul" (cf. VII:348) and as "freedom." "Freedom" was conceived as the "I-ness" that was the foundation for all things (VII:51). Hegel, for instance, took "spirit" to be a "power" that universally founds and determines everything, even nature, which is the "idea in its otherness." Goethe, for instance, in his *Wahlverwandschaften,* thought of this power as "an idea that reveals itself in various ways," in "bases and acids" as well as in human love.[19] This would be a good example of a power "behind" everything else; but it would be a metaphysical foundation, and so we must do without it here. The "essence" of a nonmetaphysical measure must rather be seen in an "appropriating giving"; and this giving itself is, as the nearing nearness and the healing force, that which gives measures in the form of love, compassion, and recognition of others. These are the measures for orienting one's conduct that we have been seeking. They are not derived from a traditional philosophy that thinks in foundationalist terms, nor are they measures from an "absolute realm," the "heavenly beings." They are measures that every path yields; they are measures that are granted to *Dasein,* which is guided from the attunement of death to an experience of the healing power. They are therefore measures that "can be experienced," and in this sense they are measures that exist "on earth."

In one of the following chapters in this volume, we will think Heidegger further in order to show that these measures have their own "sphere," a "realm" beyond and free from the occurrence of truth that is "permeated by concealment and errancy." It is only on this account that the "nearing nearness" and the healing force in its forms of love, compassion, and recognition of others can, with an absolutely effective power, exhibit the same manifestness and obligation as they did when the tradition thought of them as essential traits of a measure. The difference is that they are not transcendent with regard to those who take measure like a normative standard is, for these traits "dwell in him."

We have seen in Schelling's treatise on freedom that he determined the sphere of the absolute, the "ethical" sphere, as free from the powers of darkness that nevertheless exist within Being as such. Similarly, the calamity that reigns as nihilating Nothing may not be allowed into the dimension of the healing power as a measure. Death as a "third force" excludes it from the sphere of Being (see below, p. 110). On the level of that which is to be measured in man's soul, an "evil" lack of love intermingles with loving goodness, an "evil" ruthlessness intermingles with the goodness of compassion, an "evil" desire to dominate is intermingled with the recognition of others that springs from goodness. Nevertheless, without the measures of love, compassion, and recognition of others, man would have no means of distinguishing one from the other or for preferring one above the other. Only according to the measures of love, compassion, and recognition of others can it become apparent that there is a lack of love, ruthlessness, or a desire for domination.

One of the intentions of this chapter is to recall this one simple fact, which has nothing to do with "necessity" in the formal logical sense, but rather concerns only the necessity to act. Here is where there must be various levels of a measure that are distinct from the level of what is to be measured, and this holds for the nonmetaphysical measure of the healing force and its measure just as it does for the metaphysical measure conceived of in traditional philosophy.

A mortal can thus "take measure" again and again, he can accept or reject what he encounters as "good" or "evil" without any further reflection whatsoever. But what does it mean, then, to speak of "good" and "evil" at all; what relationship do those who take measure have to these "values" that exist on the level of measuring; and, above all, what does it really mean to "measure" if man already dwells in these measures? Before we address ourselves to these questions, I shall first attempt to respond to some objections that might arise with regard to our presentation of the path from the experience of unsettling death to the healing force. I shall also respond to some possible objections regarding our determination of the essence of a measure as a healing force in its various forms, an essence that is other than the traditional one.

Our description of the path showed that there *can* be, but not that there *must* be, such a path. For Schelling, just as for the entire onto-theological tradition, there was a measure in divine love as the "measure of man" that *must* always exist. Death, man's being-mortal, exists, and indeed, exists "forever, as long as there are human beings." However, the sudden reversal from the attunement of indifference into the attunement that eventually makes possible the experience of the healing force as a measure can take place only if a person has truly experienced within himself the transformation as a specific development. This can succeed, or, as we mentioned above, a person can also revert to indifference. He can even resist such a transformation if he wishes. The latter assumption presupposes, however, that man continues to comprehend himself as a subject in the sense conceived of in modern philosophy, as a "subject" whose 'power" shows itself in the fact that everything happens according to his "project" or plan. But has contemporary philosophy not also developed determinations for the things that "happen to us"? Our understanding of ourselves as powerful, representational subjects has been shaken not only by the structure of our understanding according to which "things happen to us." If we turn our attention from this development within the philosophical dimension and orient ourselves upon the empirical realm, we have to acknowledge developments that are being discussed everywhere. I refer to the way our world has grown so much smaller, the way that all of its inhabitants are faced with the common perils that modern technology presents with increasing urgency. It is becoming clearer and clearer that, in West and East, people are coming together in the struggle to preserve not only themselves as a species but also the natural world around them. Is it not the case that, because of an apprehension of the mortal peril posed by the threat of nuclear war, many groups in our pluralistic society are developing almost on their own into a community in which the other is no longer seen as a matter of indifference, as someone merely present-at-hand, but rather as a "comrade" whose attunement is one of solidarity? As we have shown, then, it is just a small step to the community of "thous" that we have outlined, in which we live and from which we take our measures. Is not this development, which seemed so far-fetched, already occurring, and is not a transformation taking place behind our backs, so to speak, so that all we have to do is realize philosophically that there is a measure on earth?

One could still raise the objection that the measure of the healing force and its forms as proposed here are unusual measures and that in our everyday life we are for the most part confronted with situations that have little to do with love, compassion, and recognition of others. Usually the "hard realities of life" require a "pragmatic stance." Many today may also be of the opinion that the ethics of neighborly love as it has been taught by Christianity for two thousand years has not become universally effective and therefore can hardly counter the dangers brought about by modern technology.

One can reply to these objections by pointing out that the basic determinations of a nonmetaphysical ethics proposed here are intended only as a demonstration that there *can* be measures on earth for one who has traversed this path. We have already admitted that, because it is difficult to face the truth of our Being, some people tend to flee an insight into their mortality and thus rule out the possibility that they might set out on this path. However, it does seem possible to traverse at least part of this path "collectively" with a group that has a common goal; however, if the path has not been internalized through one's own experience of mortality, it would not have the effect of changing one's character. It could well lead to utopias or to changes in social institutions, but certainly such changes would be desirable only if they could be attained without violence and with the broadest possible consensus in a democratic society governed by just laws. We shall not pursue the social and political problems involved here; but one can ascer-

tain that, in our society, there is a perhaps yet unrecognized "need"
to find an orientation for responsible action. There is a need to find
a measure that exists here "on earth." The fact that people are unit-
ing to preserve the species as a whole as well as the environment is
an indication of this. In any case, it is my view that only when man
has experienced himself on earth as a "fellow man" will there arise
a reasonable prospect of achieving what Hans Jonas proposes in his
ethics of extended responsibility, namely, that man be concerned
for those people who are not yet living with him and that he not
remain completely indifferent to what will happen after his own
death.

4. Good and Evil; Freedom

Can the traditional determinations of "good" and "evil" be reconciled with a fundamental position that is nonmetaphysical?

Good and Evil in Schelling's Thought

How did Schelling determine the meaning of good and evil in light
of the absolute measure? In the creature that is made according to
God's image, there is an ideal as well as a real power. The ideal
power realizes itself in this creature as the universal will that is directed to founding an order in communal life and thus toward the
general good. The human universal will in its turn seeks above all
to reconcile all opposition through love and thereby strives to imitate the divine measure, the "will of divine love." On the other
hand, the human will as a particular will—which is the realization
of the real power—is directed toward fulfilling the self's egoistic interest in self-preservation. Man acts "for the good" whenever he
takes care that his particular will, which is directed toward preserving his own nature, his vital corporality, is subordinated to and
pressed into the service of the universal will that is borne by reason, by a striving toward order in communal life and by love of
one's fellow man. In that case man stands in an appropriate relationship, both as a person and as a species, to the whole of Being.

The way that man, by means of his spirit [*Geist*], unites the two
wills, i.e., the one that embodies the principle of the ideal and the
one that embodies the principle of the real, depends upon the par-

ticular historical and social situation. In any case, the "good" relationship corresponds to the "divine, eternal bond of forces." The
human spirit, however, is capable of "tearing asunder" this bond.
Man can simply choose not to take measures from the absolute,
from God, and can instead make himself the measure. He is then
an "inverted God" who "skews" the relationship by subordinating
the universal will to his particular will. For the subsequent discussion it is important to see that the possibility of this skewing, this
turning of a good relationship into a bad one, was categorically determined by Schelling as the way that the real works in man; and it
is important to see that this stems from movement, contraction,
just as it does in God. Thus Schelling conceived of a necessary
emergence of evil here, provided that it moves of its own accord,
becoming more and more deeply immersed in the realm of the
dark, irrational, and disordered movement that is not banned and
regulated by the ideal forces that are directed toward the good. All
this is possible—and here it is important for our view to see
whether something is missing in Heidegger's throught—because,
for Schelling, "human freedom" exists, even though such freedom
is derived only from God's absolute freedom; man is the only creature who has been raised from the creaturely into a higher realm; to
echo Kant, man lives in a *mundus intelligibilis*. Only thus can he be
"God's representative on earth." In accordance with the human possibilities mentioned above, Schelling determines the "universal
concept" of freedom that had been conceived of in Idealism up to
that point. According to its "real and living concept," freedom is a
"capability for good *and* evil." It is within the dimension of freedom that the struggle between the human tendencies toward good
and evil takes place. Within this dimension the good must triumph
over evil again and again; it must determine itself to be in accord
with the absolute measure of "the will of divine love," so that the
"good" relation is preferred on the basis of the motive that every
creature must serve the coming of the end of the history of salvation.

Is It True That Good Is Order and Evil Is Disorder?

Can we adopt the determinations of good and evil in Schelling's
general onto-theological conception? The fact that his ethics was
based on the conviction that primordial Being is willing prevents us

from doing so. His ethics was based upon a "metaphysics of the will" and hence was an ethics of the will. For Heidegger's thinking, which was directed to the *Seinsgeschick,* this alone makes it an ethics that must be "surmounted." In our conception of a non-metaphysical ethics concerned with one's fellow man, the healing force in the forms of love, compassion, and recognition of others are also measures in which man can "dwell"—measures according to a determination of "measure" that is other than the traditional one. Here too, however, the determination of good and evil cannot be derived from a metaphysics of the will.

What about the issue that was at the base of Schelling's determinations of good and evil? This issue is the view that the "good" lies in order and "evil" in disorder. No extensive demonstration is necessary to show that order is something that is vital not only to the relationship between man's soul and his "body," but also to all human interactions. Within smaller as well as larger groups, the general understanding is that order characterizes the good and disorder characterizes evil. Today the identification of order with the good goes so far as to lead to the neglect of the following point, which I would like to emphasize as strongly as possible in this study: order is equivalent to the good in human relationships if and only if it is good in light of a measure. I pointed out earlier that especially today our experiences suffice to show that order as such cannot be the good and in this light that disorder as such cannot be evil if, as in Schelling's case, the will of divine love is no longer the measure that lends a meaning to the good and, in light of it, to evil as well.

Where does the meaning of good and evil come from for those who no longer find orientation in religious doctrines? How does one know that something is good and that something else is evil in a specific case, and in what does the motivation for preferring good to evil lie? The conclusion of this chapter until now has been that love, compassion, and recognition of others are measures according to a meaning of the essence of a measure that is other than the traditional one. If this is true, then the meaning of good and evil, as well as of what is good and evil in any specific case, must be determinable exclusively on the basis of these measures.

Here we must pause and point out a situation that is noteworthy for one who engages in philosophy in the area between traditional philosophy and a new beginning. We have seen that the values based on love of one's fellow man, which were derived from the Judeo-Christian tradition, are still valid for us today as measures with those very traits that we found in Schelling's general conception. Nevertheless, as we noted, their validity has fallen into "ruin" since, for many, the hierarchy of two levels, one of which categorially determines the Being of the divine Creator and the other of which determines that of creatures, no longer holds. As we noted above, the truth is that for the most part it has been forgotten that a measure exists at all. Hence, the difference between a measure and good and evil also comes to be concealed. The good has usurped the measure's position, though the latter must first lend meaning to the good in order for it to *be* the good. The good, taken simply as order, will result in mankind's destruction if it is not oriented upon a measure and is no longer directed toward the measure in its specific laws and rules. This can be empirically demonstrated only too well.

The concept of the good can certainly be extended so that finally it also includes that of a measure, as is the case with Plato's "idea of the good." But one cannot simply "revive" the Platonic *agathon* because we have an intellectual history behind us in which the exclusively predominant position was that there is a God who, in accordance with the traditional conception of the essence of a measure, is a normative standard for all creatures. To the extent that this conviction has lost its efficacy there is a vacuum, and the traditional meaning of good and evil, which is still valid today, lacks a source from which it could derive its meaning.

Good and Evil in Light of the "Other" Measure
and Man's "Dwelling" in Measures

The present situation demands that philosophers conceive of an essence of measure that is other than the traditional one. In proceeding from the nonmetaphysical, fundamental determination of the experience of death, we have discovered this other essence of measure in the "healing force" that we encounter in the forms of love, compassion, and recognition of others. These do not stand over against us as normative standards that place demands on us. Rather, we "dwell" within them. If the good is taken to be order and evil to be disorder, then they must derive their meaning directly from these measures. Someone who has traversed the path of experience that began in the unsettling dread of realizing the inevitability of death and then led him to be attuned to the healing force, has become a compassionate person. In a situation that concerns the "order" in his relationship with others, for example, he would actualize the good as such once he had found this meaning in the measure of compassion. It is from this vantage that he avoids or combats ruthlessness as evil. The same is true of one who lives out of the experience of the healing force and, as a matter of course, recognizes others as his equals. Since he "dwells" in this attunement, the order in his relationships with others follows from his regard for the mutual human recognition that has become completely natural to him. All of this was and is no different from the way that "neighborly love" has always been practiced in the Judeo-Christian tradition, a "neighborly love" for which the "heavenly beings" were still "man's measure." Once more, we must emphasize that the questions we have posed here concern a situation in which this presupposition of Judeo-Christian neighborly love no longer holds for some persons.

How does "measuring" take place if we have the measure on the one hand and good and evil on the other? Whoever "dwells in compassion" will experience whatever he encounters as something that is "compatible" or "incompatible" with the extent of his compassion. No explicit reflection or judgment precedes this experience, which usually takes the form of an accomplished action. The case is different whenever one provides justification after the fact for what one has done. If a compassionate person wants to be able to justify himself with regard to some previous action, then he must give an account of whether the "order" attained was truly good because it proceeded from compassion or whether it was actually ruthless and therefore evil. He will want to confirm himself in the fact that his motive for preferring good to evil was the measure of compassion within which he dwells.

Freedom as the Moral Dimension in Schelling's Thought and Heidegger's Notion of "Responding"

Is there such praxis without freedom? We have seen that Schelling was aware of a dimension within which man must make a decision in the struggle between good and evil in light of the measure of divine love. There is a "moral dimension" of freedom; this is a "fact, a feeling for which is engrained in everyone" (VII:336–37) even if it cannot be proven as a fact of reason, as Kant had seen. Do we not still recognize this fact today?

Despite Nietzsche's discovery of the power of the irrational and all that is inimical to spirit and reason; despite the antimetaphysically directed efforts of contemporary philosophy to replace unlimited human autonomy by a determination of the finitude of human Being; despite proofs given by psychology and psychoanalysis that man is dependent on irrational drives and emotions, and those given by sociology and political science that man is dependent upon social forces; despite all of this, we continue to live in the conviction that man's freedom makes it possible for him to emancipate himself from external and internal coercions and that man possesses a capability that objects and animals do not have, a capacity to relate to himself and to others, to determine himself, make decisions, and engage himself; he can experience himself as an "agent" in his actions. To use the traditional expression: man has a "consciousness of his actions" [*Handlungsbewusstsein*].

We have seen that Heidegger was influenced by Schelling's insights in the *Treatise on Human Freedom,* especially by its determination of the ideal and the real. Heidegger took the hale and the malicious to be powers of Being, but he viewed them as reigning independently of the dimension of freedom. As we have seen, he abandoned freedom, which, according to its intelligible character that surpasses anything on the level of creation, was the moment that absolutely determined the human essence in our tradition. What did he place in its stead in his later writings? If anything, it would have to be his basic determination of "responding" [*Entsprechen*].[20] We shall therefore inquire into whether this determination is not perhaps founded on a state of affairs that could be conceived of as freedom if we think it further.

"Responding" Thought Further:
Freedom as a "Latitude"

Let us first recall the way Heidegger spoke of "responding" within the "self-enactment of metaphysics," i.e., within the "domination of the essential unfolding of technology," the *Ge-stell* (cf. *TuK* 18, *19*). Someone living in this "epoch of errancy" cannot free himself from its claim, from the "call of unconcealment" (ibid.). In his labor, he discloses beings whose mode of Being is *Bestand*. That is how he "responds" to the *Gestell*. Does this disclosing that responds to the claim of the *Gestell* take place "automatically"? Labor is inconceivable without some latitude [*Spielraum*] within which the laborer deliberates and makes decisions that determine him. One who labors is engaged in what he does. At the same time, he takes a position on this or that aspect of his labor and does so through "reflections" that he determines himself, albeit in a very vague way. Above all, he is aware that it is up to him whether or not and to what extent the labor in which he is engaged will be successful. According to Heidegger's assumption, he who thus performs his labor is, of course, "blind" to the fact that he is "responding" to the unconcealment emerging as *Gestell*. He still behaves as a "subject" that, in accordance with the various determinations in modern philosophy, is credited with a capability to determine itself voluntarily, i.e., with freedom in the traditional sense.

Our question about Heidegger's determination of "responding" concerns above all the conduct of those who "open themselves to the essence of technology" (ibid., 5, *4*) in their thinking, those who are "taken into a freeing claim" (ibid., 25, *26*) and are therefore no longer blind to the *Geschick* of unconcealment reigning as the essential unfolding of technology.

These thinking persons must have "leaped out" of metaphysics, according to Heidegger (cf. below, pp. 130–34), in order to attain an "other saying of Being" (ibid.). Their disclosing in light of the "step back" also requires a "constant examination" of any further step (cf. *VA* 185); and, since these persons are called to the "guardianship of Being," it requires a special sort of "attentiveness." Is the thinking person's disclosing not based upon a certain kind of latitude, a dimension which at least in this important respect is similar to the traditional conception of freedom? And is this not also true of the mortals' response as determined by Heidegger's preparatory thinking, in, for instance, the lectures "The Thing" and "Building, Dwelling, Thinking"? Those who "dwell poetically," who are called upon by the thing, are said to "spare" the thing in the world (*VA* 179, *181*) and to "spare" the world fourfold as a whole (ibid., 159, *336*). For in order to achieve genuine sparing, must they not have distinguished between a suitable and an unsuitable means of sparing and have chosen the correct "response"? Must they not at least have been capable of rejecting a false way of hearing the call issued by the thinging of the thing?

I have uncovered the basic issue that was behind Heidegger's undeveloped determination of "responding" because I would like to think it further for purposes of our own project. But is this at all possible, especially within the framework of the determinations we developed earlier, that is, the determinations of an other essence of measure and the various forms of the healing force as the measure?

We have oriented ourselves on Schelling's determination of freedom, namely, the "moral dimension" in which there was a constantly renewed struggle between evil and goodness. However, it also contained the absolute measure of "the will of divine love" in light of which the human will that is struggling for goodness measures itself within the horizon of the history of salvation. We saw that those who dwell in the measures of the healing force, those who have been transformed into loving, compassionate persons and who grant others recognition are persons who take their measures "on earth." They measure things in light of the measures of love, compassion, and justice, and they do so with regard to what appears to them as the good, as order, and as the proper thing to do and with regard to what must be rejected as evil, as an improper lack of order. They already dwell in the realm that gives measures and yet they must continue to measure. There must be a latitude for this measuring, a latitude we may call "room for freedom."

Did not Hegel confront a similar question? He thought of "ethical life" as a realm in which the citizens of a state "dwell." For him, however, that which is "objectively ethical" was not a measure the way that the healing force is for us. That which is "objectively ethical" replaced the abstract good; it was the "living good" (*Philosophy of Right,* §§ 140, 142). As such, it constituted the order that, "if it led back to its substantial inwardness" (cf. *Encyclopedia,* 552 [appendix]), is the state. If one wishes to speak of a measure in Hegel's philosophy, it would be the "idea of freedom" as determined in its relationship to the will (cf. *Philosophy of Right,* §§ 4, 7, 10, 33), but he robbed it of its measure-giving status by equating it with the level of the good, of order. For it is a manifestation of reason, as are ethical life, the good, and order. By contrast, the realms of love, compassion, and mutual human recognition have a different status. These realms are not determined by reason but by emotions. They are not manifestations of a kind of freedom that is conceived of in terms of reason and the will.

Here freedom can be spoken of only as a "free latitude," which we recognized as the matter at the basis of what Heidegger determines as "responding." The "disclosing" conduct of one who thinks the essence of technology and spares the thing in the world and the fourfold of the world is admittedly very different from that of those who are loving, compassionate, and grant others recognition. Whoever has been transformed by the experience of death has become open to the appeal of another to act in solidarity or even fraternity and to put oneself in his place. By being wrested from their indifference toward others and by having been freed from their will to predominate, such persons have become above all else "seeing persons." They measure things in their free space with open eyes and are thus very unlike indifferent persons. Order and disorder, good and evil are something different for those who measure according to measures within which they dwell—i.e., according to love, compassion, and recognition of others—than they are for those who are indifferent to others. The freedom of those who love, who are compassionate and grant recognition to others, cannot be grasped in terms of the freedom of the will in the traditional sense. The fact that such persons already dwell in these forms of the healing force should not be taken to mean that they are determined by these forms as if by the compulsion of a drive. Rather, as the poet says so rightly, they are indeed "always aware of the right path."

In closing, we might recall once again the intention that guided Heidegger's later thinking, i.e., to save us from the "supreme" danger inherent in the essential unfolding of technology. The "lightning flash of Being" results "abruptly" and "steeply" from the very essence of concealment in this epoch of Being (*TuK* 43, 44). It grants an insight to "appropriative" [*ereigneten*] thinking and leads "preparatory" thinking of the fourfold and of dwelling in the fourfold to an anticipatory thinking of this "rescue." The determinations of nearness, nearing, and neighborhood also serve this purpose (*UzS* 208ff., *102ff.*). However, Heidegger conceived of them only in the way-making of the world play. He did not develop their implications for responsible action within the human community. But is it not really the nearness of mortals to each other in love, compassion, and recognition of others that gives hope of a "rescue"? What good would be a "turn of the past of Being into the truth of Being" (*Tuk* 40ff., *41ff.*) if it were not received by human beings who still dwelled in their faith, those for whom the "heavenly beings" are the measure, or at least by persons who are open to the healing force, so that love, compassion, and recognition of others can represent the measures that lead them toward a "conversion" in their relationship to their fellow man? Are such measures not the "saving powers" concerning which Hölderlin in his poem "Patmos," says, "But where danger threatens / That which saves from it also grows."

In our age the calamity of the loss of the faith has led to an increasingly distressful lack of orientation. On the other hand, the willingness for responsible conduct in solidarity also seems to be growing. In such an age, it is important that, in addition to Judeo-Christian ethics, a nonmetaphysical ethics can demonstrate measures that refer back to the meanings contained in this ethics. There are measures such as love, compassion, and recognition of others that exist "on earth."

The "Sphere" for the
Measure:
Surmounting Subjectivism

It is well known that Heidegger's later work is directed toward
the surmounting of metaphysics. Specifically, what must be surmounted is subjectivism in that form which, from the vantage
point of thinking determined by the history of Being, is based on
the modern principle of subjectivity. Such subjectivism is said to
have led to the "supreme danger" of today's essential unfolding of
technology, to the advent of the atomic age (cf. *SvG* 198ff.). However, for the most part it has escaped notice that the "Conversation
on a Country Path about Thinking," written in the years 1944–45,
represents an especially radical contribution to Heidegger's efforts
in this vein because it strives to accomplish such surmounting by
projecting a dimension that cannot be "characterized in terms of its
relationship to us" (*Gel* 39, *65*).

I

Heidegger gave only cryptic hints of the basic traits of this dimension. I would like to interpret these traits and shall thereby take as
our guide the question of whether or not and how they can be seen
as an effort to surmount subjectivism. It was in terms of this dimension that Heidegger determined the essence of thinking in a
manner other than the traditional one; for my part, I would like to
examine this attempt only in view of our leading question, for our
special interest is only in whether the determinants that Heidegger
unfolded for this "surmounting" might not enable us to take this

definition as the area or the sphere that might yield a measure that would show a responsibly acting person the difference between good and evil and provide him with a motivation for preferring the former to the latter.

Heidegger called this dimension as developed in the "Conversation on a Country Path" the *Gegend* or "region," and, in the older form of the word, the *Gegnet* or "that-which-regions" (39, *66*). For thinking "after the turn" this term cannot refer to the "field of vision" for the representation of objects. Nor can it refer to the horizon that goes beyond those objects or to the "transcendence" that surpasses the perception of objects. Rather, the "region" is supposed to name "that which lets the horizon be what it is" (ibid., 37, *64*). In what does the essence of a region lie if it is understood in this manner? The answer provided in the "Conversation" is that it lies in "what the open [*das Offene*] [1] around us is in itself" (ibid., 39, *66*). Heidegger had already used "the open" as a special term in the lecture "On the Essence of Truth" in 1930. There the pioneering insight so decisive for Heidegger's later thinking was that "all conduct [is] distinguished by the fact that, standing in the open, it adheres to something opened up [*ein Offenbares*] *as such*" (*WdW* 12, *124*). The open in which all conduct stands is the very open that surrounds us. This is how it was determined in 1944–45 in the "Conversation on a Country Path," where it was given the name "the region" [*Gegend*].

But how can a certain region, taken as the "open that surrounds us," be what "lets the horizon be as that which it is"? Whatever lets the horizon be cannot be restricted to a specific realm, to the particular "open that surrounds us." As Heidegger himself writes, it cannot be "one region among others" (*Gel* 38, *65*). Instead, it must be the region "in which *everything* [emphasis mine] returns back to itself" (ibid.). Heidegger thus explicitly characterizes it as the "region of all regions" (ibid.). This is what Heidegger is referring to when he states that *it* opens itself up and that the open surrounding us is *within it*.

"That-which-regions is an lingering expanse which, gathering everything, *opens itself*, so that in it openness is contained and held" (ibid., 40, *66*; emphasis mine).

I quote this section of the passage at the outset of the following

discussion because it is a guiding point for our whole interpretation. This is true even though later in the text of the "Conversation"
Heidegger failed to maintain the distinction that he himself made
between the "self-opening" region on the one hand and the "open
that surrounds us" and is "within it" (i.e., within that region) on the
other. It turns out that his failure to do so leads to an aporia. In the
course of solving this aporia, further thinking can arrive at an
"area" or a "sphere" that is suitable as a measure.

To what extent do Heidegger's determinations of the region make
it a special kind of "dimension"? Let us first consider the determination of "expanse" (ibid., 41, *67*). "Expanse means a total "openness." This entitles us to characterize the "region of all regions" as
the dimension of "openness" and to distinguish it from the particular realm of the "open that surrounds us." The "free expanse" is another determination (ibid.). The sense of the expanse as something
"free" is based on the fundamentally unboundable character of that
openness, and therefore on the fact that it is bounded by no other
power and thus extends to infinity.

It is important to recognize that these determinations of the "region of all regions" as the openness of a "free expanse" are not accessible to representational thinking. As "phenomena" they must
instead be intuited. Thus, we must envisage the "region of all regions," this "free expanse," neither as the "beautiful globe" of the
cosmos that encompasses the whole of beings nor as the limited
human world. It would be just as wrong to think of it in the modern fashion as space filled with galaxies.

Actually, we have already achieved our goal in this brief determination of the meaning of the "region of all regions," for if one
now understands openness as a "free expanse," one immediately
ceases to envisage it as an omnipotent subject thought of in line
with the principle of subjectivity. In contrast to a horizon of our
representation that can be characterized "only in terms of its relationship to us" (ibid., 39, *65*), the region of all regions can be
rendered intuitable as a realm that is "in itself" (ibid.). However,
Heidegger did not declare that the goal of the "Conversation on a
Country Path" was "to seek out" what "openness" is in itself, but
rather what the "open surrounding us" is in itself. But if the particular determinate realm of an "open" is located "within" the "region

of all regions" that opens itself up, i.e., "openness," then must the latter not also be able to be intuited as a dimension "in itself"?

In traditional philosophy, "Being-in-itself" was always the term for the unmoved *substare* of a substance. The "region of all regions" is nevertheless supposed to be intuited not as a fixed framework, but rather as a movement; and because it is just that, Heidegger called the "reign of its essence" the *Gegnende* or "that which encounters," and called the movement itself the *Gegnet* or "that-which-regions" (ibid., 40, *66*).

One of its ways of Being is, as we have shown, the "free expanse." The other is "abiding." "The region itself," Heidegger writes, is "at once the expanse and the abiding" (ibid.).

Beginning with *Being and Time,* and up until the lecture "Time and Being" in 1962, Heidegger attempted to conceive of "authentic" time as opposed to clock time. In connection with the determination of Being as "presencing" and "letting something come to presence," he conceived of essence as a "lasting" and he conceived of lasting or "incipient endurance" [*angehende Anwähren*] as "abiding" [*weilen*] and "lingering" [*verweilen*]. In the essay "The Anaximander Fragment" (*Hw* 326, *35*), "abiding" is characterized as the movement between what comes forth and what recedes on the part of something particular that abides awhile [*eines Je-Weiligen*] (ibid., 328, *37*). In the lecture "The Thing," "thinging" gathers the four-fold's "abiding" in something "particular that abides," and does so in this thing and that thing (*VA* 172, *174*). These determinations of "authentic" time as an "abiding" or "lingering" pertain to something that comes to presence, something particular that abides. By contrast, in the "Conversation on a Country Path," what is special about the "authentic time" of abiding is that it, as one of the *Gegnet's* ways of Being, is related to the *Gegnet's* other way of Being, its "free expanse."

What form does this relationship take and what is its meaning and purpose? The first thing to emphasize is that the primary issue in the determination of this attribute of the "region of all regions," namely its "abiding," is not the determination of something particular that abides—no more than it is in the case of the "expanse"—even though, in the final analysis, it is the "abiding" in its very "lingering" that allows some particular abiding thing to emerge. Later, Heidegger also tried to focus exclusively on "Being" without recourse to "beings," even though such Being is always the Being of beings (cf. ZSD 25, 24; 35, 33). Similarly, in the "Conversation on a Country Path," he conceived of the attributes of the "region of all regions" first without regard to that which finds "shelter" [*Unterkunft*] (*Gel* 38, 65) within it. This shows that the "expansing" of the "region of all regions," like its "abiding," is primarily attributable to itself and not to something particular that abides. Furthermore, it shows that both attributes are related to each other in virtue of a "movement." What is special about this movement?

We read: "It [the region] lingers in the expanse of resting. It expands into the abiding of what has freely turned back toward itself" (*Gel* 40, 66). Soon after, it is stated that "the *Gegnet* is the lingering expanse." The movement has a twofold direction here. On the one hand it proceeds by means of an "abiding" in the direction of the "expanse" insofar as it lingers in the expanse (cf. ibid.). On the other hand, however, as an "expansing" it proceeds toward an abiding. Can one say that it is this movement that first "constitutes" the dimension of the *Gegnet* as such, as a dimension that first grants "all shelter" (ibid., 38, 65)? Surely the possibility must be established that something particular that abides—"things" (ibid., 40, 66)—are able to find rest in the regioning region of all regions— "rest" in the sense of "resting" in the "abiding," of "being harbored" [*Geborgensein*] within it (ibid.).

However, there is not yet any difference between one and the other. That is why the movement can be accomplished only within the expanse and the abiding themselves; it can only be the movement of a "turning-back-within-itself." This "in-itselfness" thus establishes itself in and out of this movement as the place in which there can be a resting for "that which lingers." To put it another way, the "abiding," this "authentic" time, "schematizes" the "free expanse" that extends into infinity; it delimits this "openness" so that it "opens itself up." But to what end does the openness open itself?

I shall now quote that important passage in its entirety: "The *Gegnet* is the lingering expanse which, gathering all, opens itself, *so that* [emphasis mine] within it the open is contained and held, letting everything emerge in its own resting" (ibid.).

The finitization of the extending expanse (openness) by means of the abiding (time) that turns back into itself occurs through this "schematizing" as the region's "opening itself up" so that "within it" there can be the "open" that in turn now has its "function."

Here it is clearly stated that "openness," as a consequence of its essence, provides the realm of the "open." This realm of the open has in turn its own structure of movement with its own determinations. These, however, are so derivative of the structure of the region and its openness that as such they also remain beyond the subject's power by reason of their provenance—a point that is especially important for our question.

Before we turn to an interpretation of these determinations and the movement of the "open," the following remark should be made. It is unfortunate that Heidegger did not persist in inquiring into the determinations of the dimension of the *Gegnet,* of "openness" as such. He was too hasty in his departure from the determination of the reign of the essence of the *Gegnet* and in directing his attention to that which finds shelter within it. It will be the task of a subsequent "thinking further" to unfold the determination of the region's *Gegnet* as such with regard to its character of "in-itselfness" and the structure of its movement.

II

For the purposes of our question, it is important only to have established that the realm of the "open" stems from the "self-opening" of the *Gegnet,* the "lingering expanse." This realm is "within it" (i.e., within the *Gegnet*), as the text explicitly states. This implies that the former remains "in the service" of the *Gegnet's* "schematized openness," for the text says that the "open" is "contained and held" in it. What is it held to do? It is supposed to "allow each thing to emerge in its resting."

Here, we encounter the determination of rest in the sense of resting. But now the problem is no longer the "constitution" of "in-itselfness" from out of the movement of "abiding" and "expanse" that served to make "resting" at all "possible." Now the issue is how "each particular," how a "thing" itself attains a "resting" within the "open" provided by the region, by openness, a resting that affords the rest that is part of a "belonging" (ibid., 47, 67).

How should one think of each thing's being "allowed to emerge"

by virtue of the "open"? Is a movement of the open expanse itself
exhibited here? One will seek in vain a determination of the specific movement that "allows things to emerge" if one is referring to
the "open" as opposed to openness. Did Heidegger fail to consider
it on its own? Or did he want to express precisely that it is the
movement of the *Gegnet* itself that has the power both to grant the
open within itself as well as to assume the "function" of the open,
the function of letting each thing emerge within the open. We tend
toward the second view, for we read: "*The region* gathers, just as if
nothing were happening, each to each and each to all in an abiding
while resting within itself" (ibid., 39, *66*; emphasis mine). The
movement of the region's regioning is thus characterized as a "gathering." Not only does it "gather all" (ibid., 40, *66*), it is also what
makes each thing's resting possible. If it is the movement of the
Gegnet itself that first created in advance the possibility for such
resting—a "resting in the abiding" (ibid.)—then in the same way, it
is the "gathering" movement of the *Gegnet* that makes possible that
which allows each thing within the "open" to emerge in its resting.
It makes gathering possible as a fundamental trait of the reign of
the essence of the region itself.

In his efforts to think the "essence of essence" in an other manner, Heidegger employed recollective thought to think ahead to a
determination of the Presocratic *logos* as an "allowing things to lie
before us and as a gathering" (*WhD* 129, *213–14; 157, 144–45*). For
the most part, he thought of "gathering" as the basic trait of the
presence of what comes to presence, and did still in his final publication, *Time and Being.* He thereby viewed this occurrence of presence as occurring within the "clearing" [*Lichtung*]. In his later writings, Heidegger uses "clearing" as a terminological equivalent for
the realm of the "open." By contrast, in the "Conversation," gathering is the basic trait of the *Gegnet* itself, which on account of its
attribute of being the "free expanse" is taken to be the dimension
of "openness." Openness, which opens itself as the "abiding expanse," is what gathers in such a way that each thing, together with
each other thing, the "things" (*Gel* 42, *66*), can find shelter in the
open within it. The power of the dimension of the *Gegnet* shows
itself in its "capacity" for "gathering" each thing. According to our
interpretation, it is precisely on this account that the idea of the

gathering power of reason, which modern philosophy took as its unquestioned point of departure, was to be radically overcome in the end.

How can we determine more precisely this gathering movement of the region which is supposed to "effect" the resting of each thing within the open?

Heidegger characterized regioning [*Gegnen*] as a "gathering restoring back into the expansive resting in the abiding" (ibid.) and as the way things "rest in the return to an abiding of the expanse of their self-belonging" (ibid., 41, *67*). The question is, Whence the "*re*"-storing and "*re*"-turn? Where is it restored to? It is precisely here that one finds the clearest indication of an opposition to subjectivism such as we assumed earlier. For, in this context, Heidegger says that the movement characterized above, the movement in which each thing is gathered and allowed to emerge in its resting, has as its consequence "that the things that appear in the *Gegnet* no longer have the character of objects" (ibid., 40, *67*). Thus they not only no longer "stand opposite us," they "do not stand at all"; instead, "they rest" (ibid.). The "re-" in "restoring" and "return" refers to the way that "each thing" or "the things" *are* within the *Geschick* of modern philosophy. The power of the *Gegnet* in its gathering is capable of retrieving them from and out of their form of Being as objects. It is capable of bringing them to a "return" by enclosing them in the "abiding of the expanse" of the "schematized openness." If it is the movement within this dimension that first creates the possibility for such resting, then it is the gathering within the open that leads to a realization of this possibility. The things attain the rest that is afforded by "the lingering expanse." Heidegger later conceived of this occurrence by means of the determinations "*es gibt*" and especially "*ereignen*" (appropriating), through which each thing finds its way to what is proper to it. In the "Conversation on a Country Path" he viewed it as the occurrence of the *Gegnet*. We have seen that it is through this occurrence that the *Gegnet,* as an unlimited free expanse, "expands" into "time," into the abiding of that which freely turns back toward itself, and that within the *Gegnet* a "seat" [*Stätte*] of "in-itselfness" is established. The *Gegnet* gathers each thing into this "seat," restores or recovers each thing "back" from its Being as objectivity. It recovers them into this "seat" as the "schematized expanse" that the text also calls the "abiding of the expanse" (ibid., 41, *67*) or simply the "abiding." It is in this abiding that there is an "expansive resting" (ibid., 40, *66*).

What has only an "evanescent existence" (Hegel) in the "free expanse" as such is brought back to "what belongs to it" in the "abiding of that which has freely turned back toward itself" (ibid.) as this or that thing. In this way, Heidegger also attempts to fulfill a desideratum in contemporary philosophy: instead of the noncommital, anonymous way that the philosophical tradition, even up to and including Hegel, had ignored the individual as such in favor of the "universal," the individual is supposed to find its way to "what belongs to it."

In connection with the occurrence of *alētheia,* "disclosure," Heidegger also spoke of a *"Bergen,"* i.e., a "sheltering," "securing," or "covering." He did so in a twofold manner. In the realm of concealedness [*Verborgenheit*], of *lēthē,* there is, on the one hand, that which is covered or concealed [*Geborgene*] in the sense of something store away or preserved; that which remains covered in concealedness's keeping-unto-itself. And then there is the concealed that attains "unconcealedness" [*Un-verborgenheit*] in the movement of "dis-closure" [*Ent-bergung*]. In this movement, such things had to be "preserved" [*geborgen*] as unconcealed within the realm of that which was already unconcealed in order to be able to be a being— something that emerges in its essence. However, the "covering" that is part of in the determination "recovery" does not seem to me to belong to the matter at issue in *alētheia.* Heidegger concentrated on this issue in his later thought; his conviction was that this issue is precisely what one must think, that it is the primary aim not only of his own, but of all future thinking. Perhaps that is why he failed to pay closer attention to the movement of gathering in the regioning region. It then seems all the more important for us to prevent this thought from being forgotten, a thought that, in my opinion, could prove to be very fertile. In order to do so, we must first of all attend to the movement that, in gathering all, allows "each thing to emerge in its resting." And yet we must as a preventative measure distinguish it from the movement of the logical in the traditional sense. And second, we must positively determine the way that the regioning region is capable of this gathering as its "power."

At the culmination of modern philosophy, Hegel conceived of the movement of the concept of concepts, a movement that makes possible and permeates everything that is. He thought of this movement as a process of moving from one concept to the other, whereby the one encompasses the other as *its* "other." It is this movement of a Being-with-oneself-in-otherness that constitutes the power of the concept of concepts and this is the self-completing principle of subjectivity. Here, by contrast, the concern according to our interpretation is radically to surmount the principle of subjectivity. Therefore, the movement that gathers each thing together with the other cannot be a movement of the concept that would be comparable to the one in Hegel's *Logic*. This is precluded by the very fact that the *Gegnet* bears "everything" within itself from the outset. While for modern thinking things "stand across" [*entgegenstehen*] from us as objects [*Gegenstände*], in the *Gegnet* they are "restored back" to their own way of Being. Since the regioning region as the "free expanse" encompasses everything there is, there is no "other" in the sense of Hegel's *Logic*.

However, it only becomes clear that this cannot be a "logical movement" in the modern sense of logic if one notices wherein the "power" of the region truly lies for Heidegger. How is it that through a special kind of gathering it can, all on its own, grant a recovery and return to resting? The answer, which makes the pre-logical character of this dimension so clearly visible, is: because the power of the regioning region is that of an "enchantment" [*eines Zaubers*]. In response to the scientist's question, "What is this open expanse in itself?" the teacher replies, "It seems to me that it is like a *region,* through whose enchantment everything that belongs there returns to that in which it rests" (ibid., 38, 65). Later, the scientist remarks, "And the enchantment of this region might well be the reign of its essence, the regioning, if I may call it that" (ibid.).

Thus, it would be the "enchantment" of the region that recovers the things from their way of Being as objects, that brings them back to that which is "proper" to them, to what they "always have been."

Beginning with Aristotle's determination of substance, the philo-sophic tradition has conceived of movements that return to what has been seen from the outset as "teleological" movements of essence. The essence "plant" is realized in a movement that proceeds through all stages of being a plant, from a seed up to the mature plant, and then turns back to itself in the form of seeds. Because of the certitude with which one step follows the other in this movement's accomplishment, it could be conceived of as a "resting within itself." The movement of the region that Heidegger is thinking of here has no teleology, however. The movement back, the "re-" of the recovery, does not take place because of an essential structure in each thing that is already present. The "return" is also not a circular movement; it leads rather to a "resting" in the sense of a "belonging." With regard to this resting, Heidegger states that it is the "hearth and the reign" of all movement (ibid., 41, *61*). It is so as a "movement" that can exercise an enchanting force in a non-logical and ateleological sense. It moves by keeping to itself; it does not lose force through and in this movement, nor does it exhaust itself in its attained goal. It remains a "hearth" even in its "reign" (cf. ibid.).

Fifteen years later in his determination of an other "essence of essential being" and in the "essential being of language," Heidegger thought of this region that moves as an enchanting force. In the essay "The Essence of Language," it is stated: "The region offers ways only because it is the region. It 'makes ways'" (*UzS* 197, *92*). The word *be-wëgen* or "to make ways" means: "To provide the region with ways" or to "clear the way," and *Weg* or "way" is said to be thought of as a "letting come to completion." According to our interpretation, it is on the "way," thought of in this manner, that the enchanting force of the region proves itself. In its rest, its "self-adherence," the region is capable of recovering each thing in its resting.

In this respect, the determination of the region as an enchanting force in the "Conversation on a Country Path" also seems to have had an influence on Heidegger's later determination of the "essence of essence" and thus on the determination of the "essence of language" as well as the "language of essential being." Essence is thought of here as that which makes ways and touches us, as that which persists and concerns us in all matters. And insofar as essence is that which "makes ways for everything," we can say that language belongs to it as its ownmost (cf. ibid, 201, *95*). Are we wrong in assuming that the "enchanting force" of the region in the

"Conversation on a Country Path" is the same as what has more recently been described as the essence of language which makes ways, is at once the language of essence?

III

We must next ask how the *Gegnet* provides an abode for everything there is. How does it give things their form through the open that it opens up? How does it let the world and the thing, human Being and, in particular, human speaking and thinking, "emerge in its resting"?

Later, in the lectures "The Thing," "Building, Dwelling, Thinking," and "The Nature of Language" Heidegger recollectively thought ahead these realms of Being. However, he gives us at best only a few hints about how the determinations developed there could be thought back to the "reign of the essence" of the *Gegnet*. This is precisely what we want to attempt to do in the following pages. Only by means of such "further thinking" can Heidegger's intention become visible. This intention is to show that, like the region itself, all those realms are radically separated from subjectivity and have their real Being in the gathering movement of the region. One could perhaps express it as follows: The world, things, human Being, and, in particular, saying and thinking share in the *Gegnet*'s way of Being since they belong to it and are in it. If one were seeking an analogy to this relationship, then one could perhaps find it in the relationship of God to a creature created in God's image, as this relationship is conceived of in Christology. God is absolutely "in himself" and yet creatures "rest" "in him."

We have said that the *Gegnet* "ways" [*Wäge*] in the sense of "making ways" [*Be-wëgung*]. If the world, things, and speaking and thinking in their kinds of Being belong to the Being of the region, then they must also belong to its "waying" and themselves be "ways." This is just what Heidegger tries to show, though only implicitly. He does so by means of two determinations whose meaning becomes evident only in light of the determination of the region as we have thought it further here, i.e., as "schematized openness." One of them is the determination "nearing" and "nearness"; the other is the determination "saying." Nearing as movement and saying as movement are "the same" (cf. *UzS* 244, *107*). According to our interpretation, they are the same because they both allow the worlding of the world and the thinging of things as well as man's speaking and thinking to "emerge in their resting," and because this "emerging" is in the end nothing other than the gathering movement of the *Gegnet*. This should be shown more clearly.

1. The essay "The Nature of Language" (*UzS* 211, *104*) shows that nearness is what ways in the "mutual encounter" [*Gegen-einander-über*] of the world regions and that nearness "is, with respect to this waying: the nearing." Regarding this mutual encounter of the regions of the world fourfold, Heidegger declares: "Yet the mutual encounter has a more distant origin, it originates in that *expanse* in which earth and the heavens, God and man reach one another" (ibid.; emphasis mine).

In the "Conversation on a Country Path," we saw that the "expanse" is one attribute of the regioning region. Moreover, we also recognized that the regioning region must first open itself up in order for the "open" to come forth within it. Now it turns out that the "form" of this *open* is the world. The open—as Heidegger shows there (cf. ibid., 214, *106*)—is the "time-play-space" [*Zeit-spiel-raum*] that "temporalizing-spatializing, makes a way for the mutual encounter of the four world regions"; and these regions are the earth, the heavens, God, and man in the unity, the "play of the world" (ibid.), of "unifoldness," a unity that Heidegger explicated more fully in the lectures "The Thing" and "Building, Dwelling, Thinking."

At the end of the "Conversation on a Country Path," Heidegger expressly attempted to determine the essence of the *Gegnet* itself as the relationship between nearness and distance. Since nearness and distance cannot be outside of the *Gegnet*, "because the *Gegnet* gathers everything together and lets everything return to itself," the *Gegnet* itself must be "nearing and distancing" (ibid., 66, *86*). Heidegger restricted his comments to these hints and failed to show that and how it is the *Gegnet* that, as that which nears, allows the form of the open, the world, to emerge in its resting. In the essay "The Nature of Language," it is not the *Gegnet* but rather the "appropriating event of silence" that, in the end, is determined as that which nears (ibid., 214, *106*)—even though precisely here "world" is thought of as an arrangement of "regions." However, the determination "nearness" (in its relationship to distance) makes it clearer how the region as a power to "enchant" gathers each thing unto each other thing within itself without violating that thing's integrity.

2. The gathering *Gegnet* allow the regions of the world to emerge within the open not only as "nearness" and "nearing" but also as "saying." For Heidegger, saying realizes itself as a "showing" [*Zeige*] (*UzS* 254–55, *123–24*) and that means "to let appear, set free in clearing and concealing, i.e., to offer and extend" the world (ibid., 200, *93*). That means that it brings "things present and things absent into what is proper to each of them" (ibid., 258, *127*). We shall not delve further into the meaning of this "bringing things into what is proper to them" as the "event of appropriation" or the way that "saying moves as the showing in its act of showing." Nevertheless, this much should be emphasized: saying is what grants the "mutual encounter" of the regions of the world. To this extent, it is the "saying of the world fourfold" (ibid., 215, *107*) that "sets the world on its way" and relates, maintains, proffers, and enchances, that protects [*hütet*] "the mutual encounter of the regions of the world." Above all, it is this saying that prepares the "way" for the human speech of those who "respond" to it as "listeners." We will soon deal more closely with this way that leads to man's essence. In connection with our own theme, however, we should first emphasize something that the studies of Heidegger have not noted until now. From the viewpoint of the "Conversation on a Country Path," the nonhuman character of saying can be explained by the fact that its sphere lies within the open that is opened up by the regioning region and that saying therefore shares in the *Gegnet*'s way of Being since it belongs to the *Gegnet*. If for Heidegger that which essentially unfolds in the essence ruling language and language itself belongs in this essential unfolding that, as that which makes a way for all things, "is proper to them as their ownmost property" (ibid., 201, *95*) and if speech is a *way,* then language must belong to that which "makes ways" in the first place, and that is the region. Thus, in the later text "The Nature of Language," it is explicitly stated that "the region as a region first offers any ways at all. It ways" (ibid., 197, *92*). One can confirm that Heidegger thinks of language here

in terms of the region, for he declares that the word appears "in the region, as the region" that allows "earth and the heavens," these regions of the world, to "encounter each other" (cf. ibid., 207, *100*; 214, *106*). Our intention is to think in terms of the determinations that were developed in the "Conversation on a Country Path." Therefore, we can ascertain that saying belongs in the "open" opened up by the regioning region and that even this belonging to the *Gegnet* sets its essence beyond subjectivity. Here is where the aporia arises: that it is precisely in the essence of language as a "saying" that a "way" must be found to the being that is capable of speaking, to human beings. This certainly does not simply mean that, in the sense of modern philosophy, this being is a "subject" endowed with the "faculty" of speech. And yet the question already arises here, whether or not and to what extent Heidegger succeeded in conceiving of man's role so that man does not represent a power that is opposed to the power of the essence reigning in the *Gegnet*.

Before we turn to this question more closely, we should first examine the relationship of the gathering *Gegnet* to the things with which man dwells on this planet. As is well known, Heidegger developed the "essence" of a thing in the lecture "The Thing." The explication there has a twofold direction. One direction is the determination of a "particular abiding thing" [*eines je-Weiligen*] (*VA* 172ff., *174ff.*), a jug. Heidegger shows how the jug has its "essence" in pouring, an essence that is in turn due to the gathering of the regions of the world within this thing as well as to the movement of "thinging" that brings the regions of the world "near" to each other in it. This had remained hidden to previous thought. We cannot pursue this point in detail. What is important for our problem, however, is that in this lecture, composed five years after the "Conversation," Heidegger did not determine the movements of "thinging" and "worlding" in terms of the reign of the essence of the gathering movement of the region. This is all the more surprising since "things" were explicitly mentioned in the "Conversation" in connection with "allowing each thing to emerge in its resting" (*Gel* 40, *66–67*). The "Conversation" explains even more closely how man's relationship to a thing must be determined in terms of the regioning region. There, Heidegger shows how the *Gegnet* "conditions the thing as a thing [*das Ding bedingt*] out of and through it-self" (cf. 55ff., *77ff.*) so that the way of Being by which a thing is thought of in modern philosophy, i.e., as "*objectivity*" is overcome (cf. above, p. 81). The fact that the *Gegnet* "lets the thing abide within itself as a thing" (ibid., 54, *77*) is precisely what the expression *Bedingnis* (conditionedness as a thing) means. It is my opinion that the determinations Heidegger unfolds in the lecture "The Thing" and in "Building, Dwelling, Thinking" can be truly under-stood only if one considers the movements of "worlding" and "thinging" in terms of the movement of the regioning region that encompasses them; they are the "ways" of this movement. Further-more, one must remain aware that they find "shelter" only in the open which this movement opens up and that they belong in and to that movement.

Completely parallel to this is the way that Heidegger conceived of the *Gegnet's* relationship to man's essence as a "*Vergegnis,*" a "re-gionalizing." This point should be examined more closely here since the role and the power of man must be determined in terms of this relationship. More precisely, this is the problem that pertains to our question of whether or not Heidegger succeeded in consider-ing man's status within the whole framework conceived of in the "Conversation" such that this framework is "in itself"—"in itself" in the sense that *it* and not the subject possesses all power.

IV

In the "Letter on Humanism," Heidegger thought of the relation-ship between Being and human being as follows: human being be-longs to Being inasfar as human being ek-sists, stands out in the "clearing" of Being. By contrast, in the "Conversation on a Coun-try Path," which was written at about the same time, man's essence is determined on the basis of its relationship to the regioning re-gion. It is said not of Being, but rather of the region that it "lets" [*gelassen*][2] man into it. That is why man's relationship toward it is the "letting-be" [*Gelassenheit*] unto the *Gegnet*" (Gel 50, 74). This means that man's essential ways of Being belong in the *Gegnet* and are a result of the gathering movement in which the *Gegnet* "lets things emerge" into its "resting." This view of the status of man's essence within the *Gegnet* precludes the claim to power that was a consequence of the determination of man's essence on the basis of the principle of subjectivity. If man is let into his essence, "insofar as he originally belongs to the *Gegnet*" (ibid.), then his thinking must essentially be a "letting-be unto the *Gegnet*," it must rest on a "regionalizing of letting-be."[3] Such thinking may be said to be beyond any sort of "aggressiveness" on the part of a "subject," it is a "waiting" and a "thanking." Accordingly, the "regionalizing" of the *Gegnet* means "that our essence is let into the *Gegnet*, and indeed as thinking that belongs to it," i.e., to the *Gegnet*.

The determination of the essence of thinking thus follows consistently from the fact that thinking is one of the ways of Being to which the gathering essence of the "*Gegnet*" grants "shelter" by letting it—along with every other thing—"emerge into its resting in the open" that it opens up. Now, at the end of the "Conversation on a Country Path," Heidegger feels obliged to show what is special about man's essence. Man's essence must be allowed to be in the region, "in the regionalizing of letting-be" (50, 74) in a different manner than things are, for they are conditioned by their "conditionedness as things [*Bedingnis*]." Heidegger writes, "Evidently man's essence is let into the *Gegnet*, because man's essence belongs to the *Gegnet* so essentially that, without the latter, man's essence cannot come forth as an essence the way it does" (ibid., 62, 83). And a bit further it is stated: "the essence of man is, as the letting-be unto the *Gegnet*, used by the *Gegnet* so that this essence is regionalized and the conditionedness of a thing as such is maintained" (ibid., 64, 84).

In *Being and Time*, Heidegger had characterized *Dasein* such that it is distinguished from all other beings. Because of "understanding of Being," *Dasein* possesses at least a vague understanding of the meaning of Being—whether it is the meaning of reality or existence or of the mere "there is" (*SuZ* 7)—as well as of the meaning of its own Being. After the turn, this understanding of Being is no longer viewed as an existentiale, as a way of "Being-in-the-world." Rather, its special role in the clearing of Being is illustrated by the fact that thinking and poetizing that are "appropriated by Being" become the focal points. Man as thinker or poet is "used" by Being. The determination "to be used" is intended as a name for man's special role, but it is also meant as an indication that man, in virtue of his essence, is only a "servant" within the occurrence of Being. The determinations of the relationship between the *Gegnet* and man's essence in the "Conversation on a Country Path" are not meant to convey anything else. To be "regionalized" really means "to be used"—a determination that is not very fortunate, since it suggests a user that is substantive, and this is precisely what our thinking is supposed to overcome.

What is truly problematic and what is important for our topic is the following: by introducing the determination "*Gegnet*," Heidegger seems to have been successful in attaining a "dimension" whose character of "in-itselfness" can be determined such that all power belongs to *it*. This dimension would then stand opposed to any claim to power that would correspond to the principle of subjectivity. But then there is a contradiction when Heidegger admits "that without man's essence, this, the *Gegnet*, cannot come forth as an essence in the way it does." If man's essence plays such a decisive role, then the *Gegnet*, as the "free expanse" and the "abiding," cannot come forth "in itself" as it claims to. The only way out of this dilemma would be if it could be shown that the dependent status of man's essence, in particular his thinking, is nonetheless maintained. Heidegger saw this "difficulty" ("Conversation," 63, *84*) and tried to master it by immediately equating the occurrence of the *Gegnet* with the occurrence of truth. "We must recall," he writes, "that the *Gegnet* is presumably the concealed coming forth of truth's essence" (ibid., 59, *81*; cf. 62, *84*). According to Heidegger it is well known that this essence of truth was experienced by the early Greeks as *alētheia* but was later forgotten and concealed in metaphysics; and that he thought of it for the first time as the occurrence of the disclosure, of clearing and the concealedness that belongs to it, of the mystery and of the semblance arising from errancy. Nowhere did Heidegger attempt to demonstrate that these basic traits of the occurrence of truth are identical to what essentially comes forth in truth; later, in the essay "The Essence of Language," this does become his conviction, for there the region is determined as "the clearing that sets free, the clearing in which that which is cleared attains a free realm together with that which conceals itself" (197, *91*).

Immediately following the identification of the *Gegnet* and the occurrence of truth, there is the following statement in the "Conversation on a Country Path" that was intended as a solution to this aporia: "Man's essence is let into the *Gegnet* and accordingly made use of by it solely because man for himself has no power over the truth and because it remains independent of him" (63, *85*). The consequence is that "truth can come forth independently of man only because the essence of man as letting-be unto the *Gegnet* is used by the *Gegnet* in the regionalizing and in order to sustain the thing's conditionedness as a thing" (ibid.).

In these passages, it is at first unclear whether man's "being used" by the *Gegnet* is a consequence of his being used by the truth or whether his being used by the truth is a consequence of his being used by the *Gegnet*. In any case, Heidegger never revealed his justification for equating the occurrence of the *Gegnet* with that of truth.

The realm of openness, as I mentioned, has as its form the unity of the four regions of the world. One of these is man's essence, that in playing along in the world play has an indispensable role. The open as the world play cannot in fact "essentially come forth" unless man plays along. Man's relationship to the dimension of the openness of the region is quite different, however. The determinations in the "Conversation on a Country Path" show that man's essence is constituted by the way he relates himself to the *Gegnet* as a dimension "in itself" and that man does so "waiting" in the insistence [*Inständigkeit*] of letting-be," i.e., "thanking." He is "allowed to be" precisely because the *Gegnet* is a dimension "over which man's essence has no power." Man's "being used" by this dimension, then, has nothing to do with the "active" role that he has as one who "plays along" in the realm of the "open." If, as I maintain, the occurrence of truth itself is not concerned with the occurrence of the *Gegnet* as a dimension "in-itself" and with the Gegnet's ways of Being in its movement, then it also provides no basis for an attempt to solve this aporia. By contrast, the consistency of Heidegger's entire project in the "Conversation" would be maintained and his attempt to surmount subjectivism by means of an outline of a "dimension in itself" would be successful if the purity of this dimension's character of "in-itselfness" remained unviolated in the manner I have suggested.

We recognized that saying as a form of the reigning essence of the regioning region belongs in the region's gathering. This is the case insofar as saying, like nearing, is a waying on the part of the *Gegnet* itself and thus constitutes that which is most proper to the manner in which an "essence" ways. But we have not shown that human speaking, which is in turn "something particular," belongs in the "open" of the *Gegnet,* nor how it does so.

"Hearing" the "address" [*Zusage*] of saying is what constitutes the way; it constitutes it in the form of a bridge that connects the nonhuman occurrence of the saying (which belongs in the *Gegnet*) and human speaking. We have already said that the *Gegnet's* "waying" lets us reach what concerns us in the realm where we already reside" (*UzS* 199, *93*). The "way" that concerns us and makes ways for us must be the one that leads from the nonhuman occurrence of saying to human speaking. To put it more correctly, the way constitutes itself because saying breaks the silence and "calls." However, Heidegger himself clarified how this happens only to a limited extent. It calls to man's "listening" (cf. ibid., 180, *75*). "Listening," Heidegger writes, is "letting something be said to oneself" (ibid.). We have heard the speaking or address of language "from the outset." Reading further we see that "if we did not hear the speaking of language everywhere, then we could not use any of language's words." This "use of language" is an answer to what one has heard (cf. *Erl* 37). Consequently the way to articulated speech is so constituted by listening that the speech articulated by humans can "respond" to what has been heard. Thus it must be listening that truly characterizes man's status with the *Gegnet.* Only after he had attained this insight could Heidegger write, in contrast to his earlier position, that "the proper bearing for the thinking that is necessary today is to listen to the speaking, and not to pose questions" (*UzS* 180, *75*).

Heidegger nevertheless failed to answer our question of whether or not and how this "belonging to language" [*Zugehören*] indicates that man belongs in the *Gegnet* as it is spoken of in the "Conversation on a Country Path." The following answer might suffice: saying, this nonhuman occurrence, belongs to the *Gegnet* and is, together with it, the way to listening. Therefore, speech that is in turn bound to listening (i.e., human speech) as a "responding" must also have its "shelter" in the *Gegnet.* Indeed, all of man's ways of Being that rest upon the speaking, articulating response must be conceivable out of and in terms of the region with its attributes of being a "free expanse" and an "abiding"—even if man, in these ways of Being, is not aware of their "provenance."

Especially if Heidegger's thought were thereby successful in radically overcoming subjectivism, there would still be unanswered questions that we would have to pose on the basis of our tradition. There is, above all, the question of whether there is not a greater danger inherent in such "debilitation" of the human essence than in those consequences of the modern principle of subjectivity that Heidegger so vividly portrayed in many of his later publications.

In such a "desubjectivized" reality, there would apparently be no more room for what Kant felt as the "miracle of freedom." There would be no room for the freedom that Schelling, in his *Inquiries into the Nature of Human Freedom,* had declared to be a "fact," "a feeling for which is impregnated in everyone" (VII:336). There would also be no room for a principle that would still provide at least a foundation for man's "critical" and "moral" responsibility in the way implied in the existentiale of "disclosedness" in *Being and Time.* There would be no possibility for doubt, for examination, or for a decision in favor of one or another possibility. There would be no room for the traditional view that man has a conscience—even if only in the way that Heidegger conceived of it in *Being and Time.* Traditionally the function of such a conscience was to restrict the freedom to exercise one's "particular will"—directed as it is toward one's own interests—and to bring it into an equilibrium with one that, as a "universal will," takes account of one's fellow man, the community. Already at an early stage Heidegger had tried to "surmount" the possibility of conceiving of man's essence in terms of freedom thought of in such a traditional manner. He did so by conceiving of it in terms of the essence of truth. We just recalled his determination of truth as unconcealedness, which can be traced back to the idea of concealedness as mystery and errancy. The real objection to this way of determining truth is that it is not capable of providing a measure for responsible action and critical thought precisely because mystery and errancy are essential elements in it.

In his final essays, however, Heidegger increasingly came to think of *alētheia* as a "clearing" in which *lēthē* no longer connotes a mystery and errancy that determines clearing as a concealing. *Lēthē* now signifies the "heart" of *alētheia* (*ZSD* 78, *71*), insofar as it is a "keeping and preserving" of the saying (ibid.). *Lēthē* lies in that which remains unheeded and constitutes the history of Being. But since this has reached its end with the "entry of thinking into the appropriative event" (ibid., 44, *41*), one can say that truth as clearing comes close to being that realm that we have distinguished from the open and have called "openness," the "region of all regions." We must of course add that Heidegger still makes use of the realm of clearing to determine the occurrence of covering and concealing. And though he speaks of the "clearing" as "openness" in the same essay and even expressly calls it a "free region" (ibid., 71, *64*), he is perhaps does not mean to identify the clearing with the "region of all regions," for he does not terminologically distinguish it from the realm of the "open" as we have done. It is our opinion that Heidegger thus missed an opportunity to determine the "sphere" within which there can be a measure.

As we have said, Heidegger did not terminologically distinguish between openness and the realm of the open that it first opens up. Yet, in substance, he did come close to fulfilling this desideratum. In his explication of the poem "Andenken" ("Recollecting"), he characterized the poet's residence as the "open." It is the realm of the "between" in which God and man find their way to one another (*Erl* 139). Heidegger declares with regard to the realm of the open that it might possibly "open itself" (ibid., 140). But when does it open itself? The answer is: "The open makes itself open when that arrives which is *above* men and the gods, for in coming from high above, it *first allows an open to arise and become open* so that there can be something that is true (unconcealed)" (emphasis mine).

In our discussion of the meaning of the *Gegnet* in the "Conversation on a Country Path," in particular in view of the passage cited at the outset of this study (see above, p. 75), I insisted that there is a difference between the *Gegnet* as the dimension of an "openness" that is determined as a "free expanse" and that "opens itself up" on the one hand, and the realm of "the open that encompasses us" on the other. In our interpretation of the "Conversation on a Country Path" we maintained this distinction that Heidegger himself made

and then failed to observe. Now we see that Heidegger's own position forced him to make this distinction in this *one* passage in
which the issue is the measure for the measure-taking in recollective poetry—although he did not expressly term this realm,
which first allows the open to emerge, "openness."

How are we to conceive of measures "being given" within the
clearing thought of in this manner, within the openness of the region of all regions? Heidegger conceived of the possibility of such a
"giving" of measures in his explication of Hölderlin's famous words,
"But what remains is founded by the poets" (cf. "Hölderlin and the
Essence of Poetry" and "Recollecting" in *Erläuterungen zu Hölderlin's
Dichtung*). The poets are those who dwell poetically in the presence
of the gods and the essential unfolding of things (ibid., 39ff., 85ff.).
They "ground" the measure for *Dasein's* historical world, for poetry
is a "founding" of Being in words (ibid., 38).[4] This happens in a
"conversation" (cf. below, p. 124) in which, as an "answer" to
the "claim of the gods" (ibid., 37), something "lasting" and "long-
standing" comes to stand instead of being borne away; a measure is
placed before those who "have no measure" (ibid., 38 and cf. 90).

In his explication of the passage quoted above from the poem
"Recollecting," Heidegger comments on the determination of the
founding act in which a measure is given and notes that "remaining" by no means has the sense of a "constant presence" (ibid.,
136). Rather, it must be understood as a "going into the neighborhood of the origin" (ibid., 137), the "source"; and this source is
thought of as a "self-concealing shelter in the ground" (ibid., 138)
that leads to the possibility of "anchoring things back" on it and
thus of letting things come to the fore. In this sense the poets poetizing—as a poetical recollecting—is the "founding of that which
remains," that as the "founding dwelling near the origin," as the
original dwelling, prepares the historical site for coming to be at
home (ibid., 141).

In these remarks it becomes clear that Heidegger proceeded from
an essence of measure that was other than the traditional one. As
we have seen, however, he did not develop it. For my part, I have
not only attempted to determine an other essence of measure,
but also to exhibit the sphere where such a measure can exist,
namely the "openness," the "region of all regions." And we have

asked whether or not it is the "clearing" that, according to Heidegger's own characterization of the task of future thinking, must be thought further on the basis of the Greek conception of *alētheia*.

But how can the measure we are speaking of here, i.e., death, on the one hand and the "healing force" on the other, be thought such that they have their sphere in this openness, the region of all regions? We have spoken of death in two respects. One of them has to do with death's role within the occurrence of the totality of things. For instance, in the lecture "Der Satz vom Grund," Heidegger himself declared that death is "the unthought giving of measures on the part of the immeasurable"; the other has to do with death in its relationship to mortals' *Dasein,* the way that death extends into the *Dasein* of mortals so that it has the form of an "ongoing dying," of being able to die.

As far as the role of death within the occurrence of the totality of things is concerned, we will show that it gives the "manifestness" from which not only Nothing emerges as that which is other than all beings, but from which Being as the world essence—i.e., presencing—also emerges as the world essence. We will also show that death in this sense is what provides a measure since it is what distinguishes between Being and Nothing. Here we have seen that this occurrence must be conceived of such that death becomes manifest in the openness that comes to the fore in this occurrence; and it is this manifestness that by coming to presence and being free of all concealment plays a role in giving measures. The region of all regions, the free expanse and abiding as the "free area of clearing" would then be the enduring sphere of the measure, the sphere in which man does not stand out into Being, as he does for Heidegger, but rather into the *lēthē* that is part of *alētheia,* into death. It is in and through this standing out into death that man becomes a "mortal." This no longer has anything to do with the question concerning the role of death in the occurrence of the totality of things, but rather with the meaning of "ongoing dying." Death provides the measure with regard to man. It makes mortals open to their mortality and thus to the experience of the measure in the attunement that shows itself as the "result of the path" upon which man finds his way from the attunement of unsettling dread to that of the "healing force." What does it mean to say that the "healing force" and thus its forms of love, compassion, and mutual human recognition have their measure in the openness of the region of all regions, in the clearing? We have shown that the region of all regions, the "clearing" taken in this sense, has the character of an "in-itselfness" and thus belongs to the realm that constitutes *Dasein*'s mortality. For Heidegger clearing also has a character of an "in-itselfness" that clearly should not be understood as an ontological determination opposed to "for-itselfness." The "in-itselfness" only serves to set it apart from having an origin in subjectivity. Nonetheless, for the later Heidegger in particular it is the clearing in which man stands that must be thought of as part of *Dasein*'s "standing out into," this "ek-stasy" which, as we have seen, is based on the attunement of dread that touches one's very essence. Similarly, it is my opinion that the unsettling as well as the healing forces are not conceivable without the openness, the clearing, or the region of all regions. It is in the latter that the former have their "sphere," and it is thereby assured that the attunement of the healing force and its forms cannot be considered mere emotional processes within the subject. Rather, they are measures within which a human being who has been transformed by them may dwell.

Death and the Mortals

Heidegger took the term "the mortals" from Hölderlin's poetry (cf. *Erläuterungen zu Hölderlins Dichtung,* 60, 67). At first, it was not a term that refers to Being, such as *Dasein* did in the earlier works. It first attained this status in the lectures "The Thing" and "Building, Dwelling, Thinking." Here "the mortals" are conceived of in recollective preparatory thinking as those who can experience and think of the "world" and the "thing" in a manner commensurate with an other beginning. We will take these lectures as our point of departure.

I

"The mortals," it is stated in "The Thing," "are the human beings. They are called mortals because they are able to die" (*VA* 177, *178*). There are two answers to the question of what "dying" means for Heidegger. One of them lies in the distinction between "dying" and the way that an animal "perishes." "Only man dies. An animal perishes. It has death as death neither ahead of nor behind it" (ibid.). This answer could mislead one into referring back to the determination of dying as a mode of *Dasein's* Being as developed in *Being and Time.* There death was first distinguished from other possible forms of "coming to an end" (cf. 240).[1] The analysis of *Dasein* showed that dying is founded in care, in the whole of existence, facticity, and fallenness (ibid., 191ff.). It showed that it is part of *Dasein's* authentic potentiality for Being for it to be able to "move to incorporate" death as "its ownmost, nonrelational, insurpassable possibility" (ibid., 250). Nevertheless, the meaning of Heidegger's later determination of "dying" cannot be derived from the existentiales in *Being and Time.* It is only in the later lectures that one finds an other answer to our question of what "dying" means. "Dying means: to be capable of death *as* death." This is what we read in "The Thing," (177, *178*), in "Building, Dwelling, Thinking" (150– 51, *328*) and in other later writings, for instance in ". . . Poetically Man Dwells . . ." (196, *222*). "Dying" is this "*Vermögen,*" i.e., this capacity or capability of man. But what does a human "capability" mean after the "turn"?[2]

In the "Letter on Humanism" it is stated: "To embrace a 'thing' or a 'person' in its essence means: to love it, to favor it. Thought in a more original manner, this favoring means: to bestow its essence. Such favoring [*Mögen*] is the proper essence of enabling [*Vermögen*],[3] which can not only achieve this or that thing but can also let something 'essentially come forth' in line with its pro-venance, that is, let it be. It is by virtue of the 'strength' of such enabling by favoring that something is truly capable of being. This enabling is what is truly 'possible' [*das Mögliche*], that whose essence resides in favoring" (*HB* 57, *196*).

This passage speaks of favoring on the part of *Being,* and Being is said to enable thought such that thought belongs to and listens to Being. In this sense, Being is the enabling-favoring [*das Vermögend-Mögende*]. Our question, however, is not concerned with *Being* but rather with *death* and its relationship to mortals. And when speaking of the mortals' "own essence" (*VA* 150–51, *328–29*) Heidegger says that their essence is determined by the fact that they "are capable of death *as* death" (ibid.). It is stated even more precisely there that: "Mortals dwell in that they guide their own essence— namely the fact that they are capable of death as death—into the usage of this capability." The usage of this capability belongs to man's "own essence." In just this sense, man has the "capability" to die "continually": "Only man dies, and indeed continually, as long as he remains on earth, beneath the heavens, before the divinities" (ibid., 150, *328*).

And yet, does man have this capability on his own? When does he receive his "own essence," to which this capability belongs, and what holds him in this essence? In the lecture course "What Is Called Thinking?" [*Was heißt Denken?*] we read: "For we are only capable of doing what we favor. And again, we truly favor something only when it in turn is favorable to us, to our essential being, by appealing to our essential being as that which holds us in our essential being" (*WhD* 1, 3). In the lecture by the same name there is a similar statement: "We only truly favor whatever previously favors us on its own, what favors us in our essential being by tending toward it. Our essential being is claimed through this tending toward. This tending toward is an address. The address directs itself to our essential being, calls us into our essential being and thus holds us there" (*VA* 129, 345).

Does man thus owe this, his "own essence," this capability that leads us into this usage—"to be capable of death *as* death"—to Being? The passage quoted from "Building, Dwelling, Thinking" (ibid., 151, *139*) not only demanded that man must "guide" his own essence into the usage of this capability, but that he should guide it into the "essence of death" (ibid.); and this is supposed to occur "so that there may be a good death" (ibid.). Man is supposed to fulfill this task himself. In this sense man is supposed to be capable of death *as* death and this in turn must mean "to die continually" (ibid., 150, *138*). "To be continually dying": what else does that mean than to increasingly love "one's essence"? However, in the passage we quoted Heidegger says that Being is supposed to bring man forth in his own essence and hold him in it. We would then be confronted with the aporia that Being intends to hold man in his own essence, but that the essence of man lies in his capability of continually losing his essence. Is there any way out of this aporia? If there is, it would presumably have to be such that its outcome would be that this "capability," which constitutes the human essence, is not made possible by Being but rather by death. However, the "essence" of death would then have to connote something very different for Heidegger from the colloquial sense of the term; and the same thing would then also be true of man and his "capabilities."

II

We must therefore ask: Wherein does the essence of death lie for the later Heidegger? Heidegger's answer to this question in "The Thing" is, "Death is the shrine of Nothing, that is, of that which in every respect is never a mere being, but which nevertheless essentially comes forth, even as the mystery of Being itself. As the shrine of Nothing, death harbors within itself the essential coming forth of Being. As the shrine of Nothing, death is the shelter of Being" (*VA* 177, *178–79*).

In order to be able to understand this determination of death, we must ask first of all what Nothing means here, and second, how we should consider its relationship to Being.

Heidegger did not use the concept of "*Nichts,*" i.e., Nothing, as a special term in *Being and Time*. There he employed only the concepts "*nicht*" [not] and "*Nichtigkeit*" [nullity]. These terms are introduced in connection with the discussion of *Dasein's* original Being-guilty as thrownness (283ff.). Heidegger sees here already that the "*ontological meaning of the naughtness [Nichtheit] of this existential nullity remains obscure*" (ibid., 285). The step from the "naughtness" or "nullity" to "Nothing" as it is later carried out in "What Is Metaphysics?" must be seen as the consistent effort to elucidate this obscurity. In *Being and Time*, "nullity" is a central determination of *Dasein's* Being as care. "Care . . . is permeated through and through in its essence with nullity" (ibid.). *Dasein's* nullity constitutes its thrownness; the "guilt" of having a conscience lies in this nullity. The way that the relationship between this nullity and death is determined [4]—*Being and Time's* answer to our second question—can be seen in the fact that "care harbors death and guilt within itself in an equally primordial manner" (ibid., 306).

In his inaugural lecture "What Is Metaphysics?" (*WiM* 24ff., *95ff.*), Heidegger attempts for the first time to conceive of the "ontological" essence of Nothing in general. He does so by means of a phenomenological analysis of the fundamental determination of anxiety, because it makes the essence of Nothing accessible to experience. In anxiety we experience that "all things and we ourselves sink into indifference" (ibid., 32, *103*). "This receding of beings as a whole, which closes in on us in anxiety, oppresses us. There no longer remains anything to hold on to. In the slipping away of beings only this 'no hold on things' comes over us and remains. Anxiety reveals the Nothing" (ibid.). In the attunement of anxiety there is "not" anything that Dasein can hold on to, "not any" thing ready-at-hand and "not any" being as a whole, i.e., no context of meanings, no worldliness of the world around us in and on the basis of which *Dasein* can interpret itself (*SuZ* 87). The view that is fundamental to Heidegger's entire project is that these "phrases with existential import" only articulate what is experienced as an active occurrence in "pointing out being as a whole in its submerging" (*WiM* 34, *105*). It experiences "what makes possible in advance the manifestness of beings in general" (ibid.), a manifestness of Nothing, into which *Dasein* has "placed itself" from the outset by transcending beings as a whole in advance in order to attain its own Being-a-self and its freedom. Heidegger called this process the *"Nichtung,"* i.e., "the nihilating." He saw the essence of this "originally nihilating nothingness" (ibid.) as an active power. This Nothing is by no means the "negating Nothing in logic" (cf. ibid., 36–37, *107–8*).[5]

In order to illustrate the character of this "Nothing" as a process, it was already conceived of in the inaugural lecture as "nihilating"; and in the "Letter on Humanism" Heidegger states that it "essentially comes forth" in Being (*HB* 113, *232*). A Nothing that "essentially comes forth" cannot "exhaust itself in a hollow negation of all beings," as Heidegger declares in the Addendum to the inaugural lecture (*WiM* 43–44). It is attained by departing from the dimension of beings and is thus "what is completely other than all beings" (ibid., 45). Heidegger continued to adhere to his conviction concerning the fundamental difference between the "Nothing that essentially comes forth" and Nothing as a "concept merely opposed" to beings (cf. ibid., 35, *106*), i.e., as the negation of beings (cf. also *HB* 113, *237*). Thus we can find this view without any apparent changes in "The Thing." There, Heidegger states with regard to Nothing that it is "what is in every respect never some mere being, but nevertheless essentially comes forth" (*VA* 177, *178*).

This determination then brings us to the answer to our second question, concerning the relationship of Nothing to Being. There is an "identification" of Nothing and Being already in the inaugural lecture. Precisely because the nothing experienced in anxiety is such that it "essentially comes forth," it must "originally belong to essential coming forth itself" (*WiM* 35, *106*). Nothing "reveals itself as belonging to the Being of beings" (ibid., 39, *110*). In the Addendum, it is stated more emphatically: the readiness for anxiety allows one to experience "the wonder of all wonders: *that* beings

are" (ibid., 46–47). Heidegger stated repeatedly that his thinking
centered on just one question: What is the meaning—the truth—of
Being? The following must be added to that: from the inaugural
lecture onward, his question concerning Being was just as much
the question concerning Nothing, or more correctly, concerning the
relationship between the "essential coming forth of Nothing" that
is experienced in anxiety and the "essential coming forth of Being."
This relationship was later determined in various ways, but always
on the basis of the insight that Heidegger gained in his inaugural
lecture.[6] In the Addendum to "What Is Metaphysics?" he determined this relationship as follows: "In Nothing" one can "experience the broadness of that which gives each being the security to
be. That is Being itself" (ibid.). The determination of this relationship between Nothing and Being is spelled out in the "Letter on
Humanism": "Nihilating essentially comes forth in Being itself"
(113ff., *237ff.*); "Being nihilates—as Being" (ibid., 114, *238*); and
"what nihilates in Being is the essence of that which I call Nothing."
The consequence entailed therein is devastating for traditional ontology. It is that Being itself is finite. But is this direct transition
from the finitude of Nothing to Being comprehensible on its own?
Might one not have expected Heidegger to have drawn this far-
reaching conclusion only on the basis of insights concerning the
"essence of Nothing" in its determination of Being, insights that far
surpassed those in the inaugural lectures? There are passages in the
later writings that deal with the "essence of Nothing," but they
yield no deeper insights into the "essence" of Nothing in relation to
the "essence" of Being. Heidegger declares in the lectures on Schelling, for instance, that Nothing is something extraordinary, the most
extraordinary in the essence of Being [*Seyn*] (*SK* 122, *101*); but he
does not address the problem how such presencing in Being is to
be conceived of, in particular whether it occurs with or without
further mediation. In the Addendum to these lectures, there is the
apodictic statement: "Being is Nothing" (ibid., 228, *188*). On the
basis of the passages quoted above from the "Letter on Humanism," one could perhaps read it inversely: "Nothing is Being." In
view of Heidegger's fundamentally inimical view of dialectical
idealism, this cannot possibly be a statement that is meant to express the mediating event in a speculative sentence that would

transcend the usual form of a judgment. Should we assume that Heidegger thought of the "essence" of Being in terms of immediate "identity"?[7]

In the posthumous publication of the seminar held in Le Thor in 1969, Heidegger repeats the insight he had gained into the essence of Nothing forty years earlier. However, here the issue of how to determine the relationship between Nothing (or the Not) and Being arises in the section entitled "Being: Nothing: Same?," whereby the colon is meant to preclude the view of "identity" in the traditional sense, that is, by the copula "is." But what kind of identity is meant here?

In response to this question, we shall turn to an interpretation of the passage quoted above from "The Thing," for our thesis is that here Heidegger came to a new view concerning the relationship between Nothing and Being and that he projected a role for death in this relationship. I must immediately add, however, that he did not make this projected role of death explicit, nor did he demonstrate what consequences follow from it. This is what we, in thinking Heidegger further, shall attempt to do here. For it is my opinion that, even if only cryptically, he embarked on a new path here. On this path, not only is the "ontological" problem of the relationship between Nothing (the Not) and Being determined in an other manner than before, but a meaning is also ascribed to death that has not been recognized until now. In order to show this as our next step, we shall return to the question of where the "essence of death" lies for the later Heidegger. We will see that the completely different meaning of death simultaneously sheds new light on the "essence of man" and thus on that being to whom Heidegger gave a new title in view of its Being, i.e., "the mortals."

In line with this thesis, we then ask how Heidegger projected the role of death in the relationship between Nothing and Being. At first glance, it seems that he simply "identified" death, first of all, with Nothing's essential unfolding and, furthermore, with Being's essential unfolding. For, on the one hand, he determined death as the "shrine of Nothing" and, on the other hand, he declared that this shrine harbors "within itself *Being's* essential unfolding." It is said to be the "shelter of *Being*" (emphasis mine). But do these "identifications" express an immediate identity? They certainly do not.

Death is determined in its relationship to Nothing as well as to Being by means of the image of a "shrine," and thus by means of that basic trait which, according to Heidegger, "mediates" everything there is, namely, *alētheia*.

III

We do not have to retrace the development of the determination of *alētheia* in Heidegger's thought. It suffices to recall that, soon after *Being and Time,* Heidegger conceived of the matter at issue underlying *alētheia* as "the occurrence of a clearing" that opens up "an open space in the midst of beings" (*Hw* 41, 52; 43, 54); a clearing within which there is a coming to presence of that which is present and a coming to be absent of that which is absent. Such "clearing" should not be thought of statically. Clearing is the unconcealedness or disclosure reigning in the occurrence of coming to presence, out of which that which is present emerges in its presence and into which that enters which was already unconcealed. Hence, concealedness, the *lēthē,* also belongs to this unconcealedness. At an early stage Heidegger had already called it the "mystery" (*WdW* 21, 132). As opposed to that which is present, this occurrence of coming to presence itself remained concealed to thought—especially the emergence due to unconcealedness, due to the clearing, and the entry into the clearing. This concealedness, the clearing's self-concealing, belongs to the *Geschicke* sent to Western thinking; it belongs to the history of Being, which, according to Heidegger (cf. *ZSD* 44, 47), first begins to be transformed when an insight into this occurrence is dispatched to his thinking.

As his thinking developed, Heidegger increasingly came to attribute the power that is active within the whole occurrence of *alētheia* to the *lēthē.* In the end, he saw the latter as the "heart" of *alētheia* (cf. ibid., 75, 68; 78, 71), that which is most proper to it, that which as "the sphere of stillness gathers within itself what first grants unconcealedness" (75, 68). The *lēthē,* the mystery, is, on the one hand, the fact that the *Geschick* keeps to itself; on the other hand, however, it is "not merely a self-closing, but is also a harboring [*Bergen*] in which the essential possibility of something emerging is preserved. . . . Self-concealing [*Sich-verbergen*] guarantees [*verbürgt*] self-disclosure [*Sich-entbergen*] its essence" (*VA* 271, 224). This gathering harboring (ibid., 256, *101*) and the particular disclosure that emerges from it is therefore "what is to be thought" by man so that man may accept the "disclosing" "in response to" the particular *Geschick* of disclosure, of clearing, sent to him.

Out of all the various kinds of concealment, there is one that gathers the "utmost concealedness of Being within itself."[8] This is death (*UzS* 23, 200), and it is for this very reason that Heidegger conceives of it by means of the image of a "shrine" in the lecture "The Thing." This means that death is as such *lēthē;* but it is not only as such *lēthē*. As the "shrine *of* Nothing," it is also the *lēthē* of Nothing. Nothing is therefore *lēthē,* the mystery, only because and insofar as it is a form of death. Death is the form in which Nothing confronts man. It confronts him specifically in the anxiety arising in the face of death, a conviction that Heidegger already held in *Being and Time* and also, though no longer explicitly, in "What Is Metaphysics?" At that point, Heidegger was convinced that man can uncover the essence of Nothing, which confronts man in anxiety as "what is other than all beings," as the "veil of Being" (*WiM* 51). The later Heidegger, however, no longer seems to be of this opinion. Nothing holds itself back in unveiling its essence, for it is and remains *concealed* in its "shrine," in death. Although Nothing is still *lēthē,* "the mystery of Being itself" (*VA* 177, *178*), it is so only in a "derivative" way—a point that should be kept in mind. Death is what constantly keeps the Nothing concealed, and this implies that death, as that which conceals, is in a proper sense and as such *lēthē*.

But does death, the shrine, essentially unfold only as *lēthē, only* as the mystery? Does *lēthē* not essentially belong to *alētheia,* does concealment not essentially belong to unconcealedness? Insofar as both Nothing and Being still keep their essences to themselves, there may be a reason to "identify" the two. Yet, if death as opposed to Nothing is as such *lēthē,* as we have shown, then it alone is what gathers as the heart of *alētheia*. It alone "grants" unconcealedness, the clearing of the open, and disclosure. Then it alone is, as Heidegger writes, "the supreme shelter of Being" (*VA* 177, *178*)[9] and is as such "the mystery of *disclosure* in its calling" (ibid., 256, *101*; emphasis mine). By contrast, since it is only a derivative form of *lēthē*, Nothing does not grant *alētheia*, the clearing of the open and the disclosure of the Being of beings as a whole.

In "What Is Metaphysics?" on the other hand, Heidegger ascribed an "essentially unfolding power" to the Nothing that is experienced in anxiety. He did so precisely because the Nothing "makes possible" the "original manifestness" of beings for human *Dasein*. It makes possible an insight into the wonder of wonders: *that* beings *are*. What makes the manifestness of beings possible is the Nothing into which *Dasein* has extended itself in advance in order to transcend beings as a whole. It is important to note the following: first of all, the later Heidegger's concern is not the manifestness of beings as such, but rather of the Being of beings as such (or of the presencing of that which is present). This manifestness is no longer made possible by the "nihilating Nothing," but rather by the "supreme shelter of the mystery of *disclosure* in its calling" (emphasis mine), i.e., by death. Furthermore, it is only by virtue of this disclosure, this manifestness, that Nothing itself can also be experienced as "that which is other than all beings"—as the essentially unfolding Nothing. If death is now not only the mystery but, as such, is precisely the "mystery of disclosure in its calling," then our preliminary assumption is refuted and death's essence cannot be "identified" with that of Nothing.

If death is the "shrine" or the "shelter" of Being, then this implies that it is not as such "identical" with Being. Death, even if it is projected as being part of the relationship between Nothing and Being, has as such an other essence than Nothing and Being. It is *other* than either of them.

Thus, our attempt to think Heidegger further indeed leads us to a very decisive consequence as a result of our attempt to redetermine the relationship between Nothing and Being. As a third element in this relationship, death is a "power" in its own right with its own meaning. How can we determine what this meaning is, if our view is directed neither to the death of an individual *Dasein* that is singularized by death (as is the case in *Being and Time*) nor to the mortals' relationship to death as it extends into their *Dasein*, but rather is directed to death's status as a power of Being within the whole framework (such as Heidegger spoke of it in *Der Satz vom Grund*, for instance [186–87])? We recall that, in his last statements,

Heidegger declared that Being and Nothing were "the same" (*Vier Seminare*, 99). How are they or how do they become "the same"? Our answer is that they do so by both relating themselves to death. To be the same does not mean to be identical. It means to be "akin." On what can kinship be founded? It can, for instance, be based on the fact that one thing serves two others and does so in the same way. Nothing and Being exhibit a relationship of kinship to one another because—and this is our thesis—death "serves" both of them in the same way. First of all, death serves both in the same way since, as the heart of *alētheia*, as the mystery of disclosure, it grants clearing, grants unconcealedness not only to the essence of Nothing but also to Being, as we have already seen. It grants unconcealedness to Nothing, so that from and within this unconcealedness, it can appear as that which is "other than all beings." In the same way, death grants disclosedness, unconcealedness to Being (presencing) so that Being can emerge out of it as the essence of the world. In precisely this sense, death is capable of the "utmost in the clearing of Being and its truth" (*SvG* 186–87).

Death as the "mystery of disclosure in its calling" furthermore serves both Nothing and Being in the same way and thus makes them akin by lending them *its own* character as a mystery. We have already shown that the essential unfolding of Nothing appears by confronting us in the form of the shrine, as death. In precisely this way, Nothing receives its character as a mystery from death. However, Being (presencing)—the essence of the world—also receives the character of a mystery, for the unconcealedness into which it emerges remains permeated by concealment, and this concealment is gathered about all in death. The "essential unfolding of Being" indeed remains harbored in the shrine of Nothing, namely death (cf. *VA* 177, *178*).

However, it also belongs to the essence of death as "that which grants," to grant manifestness and the character of "mystery" to Nothing, on the *one* hand, and to Being on the *other*. Death thus "makes a distinction," and it grants *Dasein*, to which it relates itself, the possibility of distinguishing between what is and what is not. In the face of death, even if one takes death as the "utmost shelter of the mystery," man experiences this difference. As the mystery of "*disclosure* in its calling," it is precisely this distinction that, in its

call to *Dasein,* discloses itself to *Dasein* as the decisive distinction.
And is there not something else that also discloses itself to *Dasein*
precisely in the face of this mystery? We shall return to this question at the end of this chapter.

We thus think Heidegger's determination of death further, so that
death both grants Nothing and Being the possibility of disclosure,
manifestness, as well as lending them the character of a "mystery."
It is thus a third force over against Being as well as the nihilating
Nothing. This is the only way to determine suitably its "role" or
"function" as "something that grants." As a third force, death "is" as
the distinction; that is, it "is" as something that separates nihilating
Nothing and Being. It cannot be emphasized strongly enough that
we are thereby departing from Heidegger's position, according to
which "Nothing occurs in Being itself" or "Being nihilates—as
Being" (cf. *HB* 113–14, *237–38*).

This also implies for us now that, in the mortals' relationship to
death as it is embedded in their *Dasein,* in their experience, one
must make a fundamental distinction between the "supreme concealment of Being," i.e., death, and the "supreme disclosure of
Being." It is death in its distinguishing function that in turn grants
Dasein, which by "continually dying" relates itself to death, the
possibility of distinguishing between what is not and what is.
In the face of death—taken in Heidegger's sense as the "supreme
shelter of the mystery"—man also experiences this distinction
that, in calling to *Dasein,* discloses itself to *Dasein.* We have also
thought Heidegger's determination further in a manner such that,
in the clearing that disclosure grants, *Dasein* experiences that which
reigns as nihilating Nothing, the calamity that unsettles everything
meaningful, in the attunement of unsettling dread. However, man
also experiences the very repulsion [*Abstoß*] from it; he experiences
the "supreme manifestness" of Being, the healing force. Man experiences it in an openness that is nevertheless permeated by the
mystery whenever he has become a "mortal who plays along" in
the playing of Being.

IV

We thus come to the central question in this essay: Who are
the mortals? Up until now we have replied with the answer that

Heidegger himself gave: "The mortals are the human beings. They are called mortals because they can die. To die means: to be capable of death as death." This capability is said to belong to man's "own essence." Since after Heidegger's "turn" man has his "own essence" in virtue of the "clearing of Being," we concluded at first that it must be Being that enables man's own Being in the sense of "favoring it," so that it holds man in this essential being. In "Building, Dwelling, Thinking," however, it is demanded of man that he guide his "own essence" into the usage that belongs to it, and thus into the essence of death "so that it may be a good death." This is what Heidegger calls "continual dying." We pointed out the aporia in this passage: on the one hand, Being is supposed to hold man in his essence, while, on the other hand, man loses his essence in his continual dying. We expected to find a solution to this aporia in the fact that Heidegger associates a completely different meaning with death, dying, and the "essence" of man than the usual one. In the meantime, we have shown that this is indeed the case. Heidegger even expressly demanded that man abandon his self-understanding as an *animal rationale,* which has dominated the whole of metaphysics (*VA* 177, *178*). Indeed, it may be the insight into the completely different essence of death that forces one to abandon the form of man that has decayed[10] (*UsZ* 46, *168*). But what new form of man's essence emerges if man abandons the one that has "decayed," i.e., if man has departed from the form that is corporeally bound and is determined to be outlived and to decay? What new relationship between death and man shows itself if death is grasped as a power that, according to our interpretation, grants both manifestness and the mystery to Being as well as to Nothing. How are we to conceive of the relationship between human beings' essence and the power of death thought of in this manner such that the humans are "mortals"?

The question concerning this relationship has to do with those human beings for whom death is no longer what brings about the deterioration of their bodily form and no longer externally confronts them as the end of their lives. Already in *Being and Time,* death accrued to *Dasein* as one of its "possibilities." We recalled that *Dasein,* as potentiality-for-Being, could anticipate death as an insurpassable possibility. In so doing, *Dasein* could "conclude" this potentiality as a whole. Now man's relationship to death is thought of "inversely," as that of death to man. Humans "are" or "have their essence" *in* death as the "gathering recovery," the "shelter." They no longer stand over against death so as to be able to anticipate it as that which comes toward them, but rather they find their place *in* it.

In the "Letter on Humanism," Heidegger determined man's "essence" in terms of man "ek-static instanding" (*HBf* 74, *210–11*) into the "clearing of Being." Man's essence belongs in the essence of Being because man is "the '*Da*,' that is, the clearing of Being." By means of this very insight, Heidegger attempted to surmount the old concept of the "essence of man." Nevertheless, the quotations from the later lectures that were cited at the beginning of this chapter give one the impression that Heidegger reverted to this older concept. It is precisely this appearance of a recourse to the old concept that led to the aporia we pointed out. The solution to this aporia has led us to the insight that man's essence does not lie in his standing out "into the clearing," the *alētheia* of *Being*. It lies rather in his standing out into the *lēthē* that belongs to *alētheia*, into *death*. Man stands out into death by experiencing it as "the supreme shelter of the mystery of disclosure in its calling." As we have shown, this means first of all that man experiences death as the power that gives standards insofar as it is a distinction that grants to the essentially unfolding Nothing and Being the unconcealedness, the manifestness in which they emerge. Second, it means that man experiences death as the power that gives the essentially unfolding Nothing and Being the character of a mystery. Only when human beings have experienced this power in death in the twofold directions that give measure can they "become" mortals. Then they can fulfill the role that has been allotted them because they alone "belong" to death; and, by virtue of death's measure-giving "mediation," they then belong to Nothing and to Being. This "belonging" can be thought of in terms of the event of appropriation, the key term for the later Heidegger. As those who are "delivered over" [*Zugeeigneten*] to death, and who by means of death are delivered over to Being and Nothing, they are those who have been "appropriated" [*Ereigneten*] by death.[11]

If man's essence lies in this belonging to and being delivered unto death, then what it means to be capable of death *as* death will follow from "man's own [*eigenen*] essence." This means that man is capable of fulfilling the role alloted to him, i.e., of listening to the "supreme shelter of the mystery of disclosure in its calling" and of responding to what he has heard. But what does such responding entail?

Here we must recall that the passage we have just interpreted is located in the lecture whose topic is the "world" and its relationship to the "thing." We should also recall that in the lecture "The Question of Being" Heidegger crossed out Being, which was supposed to point "to the four regions in the fourfold and their gathering in the point that is crossed out" (31, *83*). For the later Heidegger, "Being" is synonymous with "the essence of the world."[12] We shall not discuss here that and how the "essence of the world" as the "ringing of the mirror-play" can be experienced in the "nearing" of the four regions of the world in the "thinging thing," for instance, in the pouring of a jug. All that is important for us here is that the "condition for the possibility" of this experience is that the "rational animate beings" have *become* mortals (*VA* 177, *178*). They have become mortals, however, only when they "knowingly dwell in death," as we have seen, when they experience it as the "supreme shelter of the mystery of disclosure in its calling" (ibid., 256, *101*) by listening to this call of disclosure. The appropriate listening is only possible, of course, if one has surmounted the attitude of "representational" thinking and the "presumption of any unconditionedness" (ibid., 179, *181*) made by the *animal rationale,* especially as thought of in German Idealism. After man has taken the "step back" from representational thinking, he attains that "recollective thinking" that has its abode "in the essence of the world" within which man is addressed by this essence and "answers" it. Humans, "mortals"—not in the sense of just *one* among the other regions of the fourfold[13]—can do so, however, because they stand out into the mystery of death and its disclosure in calling.

They "die continually" or "are capable of death as death" if they listen to death as the "mystery of disclosure in its calling," if they accept death as the "envoy" of Nothing which confronts man in the form of death, to use a phrase from "What Is Metaphysics?" (38, *108*). Man is "capable of death as death" if he "holds it open as the sphere" (cf. *Zur Seinsfrage,* 38, *97*) that gives unconcealedness, manifestness. It is the sphere out of which not only Nothing emerges as "that which is other than all beings," but out of which presencing as the essence of the world also emerges and *allows* that which is present, especially the "thing," its "thinging," to be. This is the "condition for the possibility" of the recollection of the "world and the thing." On the "pilgrimage toward death" (*US* 23, *200*), the willingness thus grows to listen to the mystery, to death as "disclosure in its calling." Hence, by "having one's essence in the shelter of Being," in the utmost shelter, in the "gathering recovery" (*VA* 256, *101*) that grants emergence into the disclosure of Being, man is increasingly willing to let Being be *as* Being, as the essence of the world in its "worlding" and "thinging." By listening in this manner, "mortals" are the "essentially unfolding relationship of Being as Being" (ibid., 177, *179*). This is the meaning of the last sentence of the passage.

Heidegger sees "the rescue of man's essence from the danger reigning today" in the expectation that "when, all of a sudden presumably, the world worlds as world" (ibid., 180, *182*) humans will find their way out of the domination of the essence of technology into the primordial form of human Being. This would be the "locality" [*Ortschaft*] of the human essence" (*UzS* 190, *85*) that is so proper to mortals (cf. ibid., 259, *128–29*) that one can say that "we already have our abode" (ibid., 12, *190*) in it, and that means to "dwell poetically." But this transformation can come about only if "the rational animate beings" have *become* "mortals." "Men alone, as mortals, by dwelling attain to the world as world" (*VA* 180, *182*).

Wherein lies the completely different meaning of death which, we declared, had not been seen previously? The first thing one must realize is that the issue is death as it can be experienced by man during his *Dasein,* death as the "utmost possibility of mortal *Dasein* and not the end of what is possible"; the issue is death in relation to *Dasein* and thus by no means death as the end of life (cf. ibid., 151, *329*). To this extent, Heidegger's position does not appear to have changed since *Being and Time.* One important difference from *Being and Time,* however, is that the issue is not one's "ownmost" death, which can be existentially experienced and determined as an existentiale; the issue is not death as it thrusts *Dasein* back upon itself, individualizing *Dasein* in the uncanniness of its "existence" when it anticipates death. After the turn, the relation-

ship of *Dasein* and death—as well as Being—must be thought of
"inversely." Death must be conceived of as the power that extends
into *Dasein* and decisively sets standards for it and founds *Dasein's*
relationship to it. That is why Heidegger can also speak of death as
a power "in itself," as he does for instance in *Der Satz vom Grund,*
where he determines human beings as "mortals" because they
"dwell in nearness to death" (186). That is why he declares in "Language": "Death has already surpassed any dying" (*US* 23, 200). The
view of death as a "power in itself" corresponds to the idea that is
expressed in the colloquial meaning of death that sees it as an absolutely uncontrollable "power" that we fear or within which we try
to find our peace. In any case, the inversion in the relationship of
death to *Dasein* comes much closer to prephilosophical experience
than did the relationship between the two in *Being and Time,* which
was thought of as the relation of *Dasein* to death.

What is so completely other in the meaning of death lies in the
fact that, on the basis of this inversion, death must be conceived of
as an occurrence to which man owes his "essence." The role that
death is thus given according to our interpretation is admittedly
enormous, for if death is what grants disclosedness, manifestness,
then it is because of death that man is *as* man, for without death
there would not be the "determinations" that appear to human experience only within this manifestness and provide the basis for all
understanding and speaking. There would be no understanding of
Being and of Nothing, of world and thing; man could not think as
man; without manifestness, there would also be no thinking that
has been "appropriated" by Being.

The role of death is also so important because it grants Being and
Nothing the character of a mystery; and, in Heidegger's view, it is
only the experience of the mystery that gives us any promise of a
"rescue." In a manner similar to the way that some religious views,
full of trust and hope, see death as the "realm" into which the soul
that has been freed from its body will enter, a realm that man can
relate to in his fate during his lifetime—so too is it part of the "essence" of mortals for Heidegger that they stand out in the mystery
as a possibility of *Dasein* and that they dwell at the source of what
arrives as disclosure. In "continually dying," mortals are capable of
hearing the call of the mystery's disclosure, which makes the recol-

lective thinking of world and the thing possible. Thus, finding their essence in the "shelter of Being," mortals are familiar with the dimension of the *lēthē*. That is why as thinkers they can take on "the task of thinking at the end of philosophy," i.e., attend to death "as the covering and securing" "out of which disclosure is first granted and out of which that which is present can thus appear in its presence" (*ZSD* 78, 71). They "who tread dark paths" (*UzS* 23, 202) can recollectively think ahead to the possibility of "dwelling poetically."

That is why "the essence of mortals" today is already "called to attentiveness toward the calling . . . that calls them to come into death" (*VA* 256, 101), into *that* death to which man owes his human Being and, perhaps one day, his rescue.

In closing, let us add the following steps in a further thinking by asking the following: If death is that which is "other," over against Being and Nothing, what does that indicate? We have not taken death to be the "deterioration of the body," but rather we have followed Heidegger in viewing it as the "utmost shelter of the mystery of disclosure in its calling" and have conceived of it as the "supreme *concealment*" of Being. Can we not presume then, that what "death as this mystery calls into the disclosure" is for its part the "supreme *disclosedness*" and that this is in turn also "something other" than Being and the Nothing within Being? Can we not presume that this "something other," since it belongs to another dimension, has its own "sphere" as opposed to that of the occurrence of Being, i.e., the occurrence of truth, and that this is where there is a measure or measures?

In the preceding chapters, we discovered that what is "lacking" in Heidegger's entire project is that there is neither a "sphere" free from concealment, errancy, withdrawal, and danger, nor did Heidegger conceive of the measures that would reign in such a sphere. We have thought further the "region of all regions" as such a "sphere" in which a measure holds and we have called this measure the "healing force," a term we also applied to its exemplary forms of love, compassion, and mutual human recognition.

The mortals are those who have learned to be capable of death as death, who are "continually dying" in the sense we have described. Can one not say that during and not just at the end of their

Dasein, mortals can experience the existence of measures? As we have shown, Heidegger himself did not describe the attunement in which mortals are capable of death as the "shelter of the mystery of disclosure in its calling." Are they capable of it in that basic state of mind that was pointed out in the analysis of *Dasein* in *Being and Time,* i.e., in anxiety, an attunement that was made possible by *Dasein's* anticipation of death? For Heidegger after the "turn," it was "essential anxiety" that made possible the "wonder of all wonders," Being, and not the experience of death (Addendum to *WiM* 46–47); perhaps this "essential anxiety" also made possible the willingness to let death be as death implied in the idea of "letting be" [*Gelassenheit*].

But must not a mortal whose attention is directed to death first experience that what increasingly forces his existence into absence, into departure, is something "unavoidable" and "horrible," that it is dreadfully unsettling for a being that seeks to preserve life and meaning to be caught up in the attunement of terror, of unsettling dread? And could this experience not lead to a transformation in a mortal's existence, a transformation that would gradually change one's relationship to oneself, one's fellow man, and the things around one so that the attunement of the "healing force" would arise out of that of unsettling dread?

By thinking Heidegger further, we have shown how, out of this sudden change in attunement, the attunement of the "supreme disclosure" can come about, the attunement of gratitude. Mortals can experience the healing force in the measures of love, compassion, and mutual human recognition, measures that form their lives, because they have experienced death as death, experienced it with dread as an unsettling calamity. This is the only way that a transformation of their whole essence is conceivable. Hence, it is death that in the end makes mortals open to the experience of measures in which they learn to "dwell" and in light of which they can distinguish between the "appropriate good" and the "inappropriate evil" and find a motivation for preferring good to evil.

Death and Language

In the lecture "The Essence of Language" we read: "Mortals are those who are able to experience death as death. Animals cannot do so. But animals cannot speak, either. The essential relationship between death and language flashes up before us, but remains yet unthought. It can, however, give us a hint about the way that the essence of language reaches out and concerns us, thus holding us in relation to it, in the event that death belongs together with what reaches out and concerns us" (UzS 215, *107*).

For my part I would like to try to take a Heideggerian viewpoint while intentionally proceeding beyond him in thinking the essential relationship that remains as yet unthought by him. In order to do so, we must first bring into view how he viewed the one side of this relationship, the "essence of death," and the other side, the "essence of language," in his later work. Going further, we shall deal with the determination of the essential relationship between these two sides. We will proceed from Heidegger's assumption "that death belongs together with that which reaches out and concerns us" and that "the way it reaches out and concerns us" is indicative of the way that the essence of language reaches out and concerns us.

I

Although in his early writings Heidegger dealt with death only in view of *Dasein's* relationship to it, in his later writings—his thinking "after the turn"—he determined this relationship by proceeding from the essence of death with regard to those humans who have "become mortals."

In the essay "The Thing," Heidegger determined the essence of death as follows: "Death is the shrine of Nothing, that is, of that which in every respect is never a mere being, but nevertheless occurs even as the mystery of Being itself. As the shrine of Nothing, death harbors [*birgt*] within itself the essential unfolding of Being. . . . Mortals are who they are, as mortals, by having their essence in the shelter of Being. They are the essentially unfolding relationship of Being to Being" (*VA* 177, *179*).

Death is thus conceived of by means of the image of a shrine (cf. above, p. 107). According to our interpretation, the image of a shrine expresses the structure that for the later Heidegger reigns in everything there is, i.e., the *alētheia* structure. It is an expression of the occurrence that, out of the realm of *lēthē,* concealedness, and mystery grants disclosedness for the coming to presence of that which is present. Death is the "supreme concealedness of Being" (*UzS* 23, *200*). As such, however, it is not thought of as that power that results in the body's decomposition (cf. ibid., 46, *167*), but rather—completely in line with the meaning of *alētheia*—as the "supreme shelter of the mystery of disclosure in its calling" (*VA* 256, *101*). Humans are "mortals" to the extent that they stand out into this gathering, securing force [*Bergende*], this "shelter of Being"; they are mortals to the extent that they can thus listen to the "call" of the occurrence of disclosure or coming to presence and can respond to it. To this extent, they are the "relationship of Being to Being." If, out of this relationship, they "let" the world "world" and the thing unfold itself in its "thinging"; if this takes place from an experience of the mystery; and if they stand out into death in this way (cf. above, p. 112); then they experience death as death, as is stated in the quotation we cited at the outset.

What we have said up until now about the determination of the essence of death in its relationship to mortals does not tell us anything about its "essential relationship" to language. In particular, one cannot recognize what it means to say "that death belongs together with what reaches out and concerns us." However, we shall leave this question open for the moment and turn to the other side of the as yet "unthought essential relationship," to the essence of language. Here again we shall restrict ourselves to the one aspect that is important for our theme.

II

How did Heidegger conceive of the essence of language, the saying [*die Sage*]? As the quotation cited at the outset states, one must proceed from the assumption that one of its basic traits is that it "reaches out and concerns us and thus holds us in relation to it" (cf. above, p. 86). What does that mean? The essence of language for Heidegger is saying. He takes saying to be a nonhuman occurrence. It is one of the "ways" that follows from the freeing-sheltering character [*dem Freigebend-Bergenden*] of the "region" [*Gegend*] that "regions" [*gegnet*] by setting us under way [*uns be-wëgt*] and reaching out and concerning us (cf. *UzS* 171, *68*; 197, *91*; 201, *95*; and above, p. 86). Saying as a "way" [*Wëg*] is the "essence" of language, whereby "essence" is thought of in a manner other than the traditional one, namely as "that which persists," that which "concerns us" since it sets everything upon its way (cf. ibid., 201, *95*). Such a view of the "essence of essence" suffices to explain why, in the quotation cited at the outset, Heidegger proceeded from the assumption that the essence of language, saying, reaches out and concerns us as an essence.

What does the phrase "to reach out and concern us" [*be-langen*] mean more exactly? Heidegger declares that "what concerns us" [*Be-lang*] is what "reaches out [*auslangend*] after our essence, issues demands [*verlangt*], thus letting it reach [*gelangen*] to that wherein it belongs" (ibid., 197, *91*). It is that which "the concealed realm of language holds in store in order that these riches may reach out and concern us for the saying of language" (ibid.). Is this his whole answer? It tells us nothing about whether or not and how the essence of death and the essence of language belong together such that one can speak of an "essential relationship." In what can Heidegger have seen this essential relationship? As he declares in the quotation, this relationship is as "yet unthought" but nevertheless he assumes that it exists, since it is capable of giving us a "hint" of the way that saying reaches out and concerns us.

III

Already in *Being and Time* Heidegger had named one of the determinations of the "meaning of Being" that he sought there, the "*es
gibt.*" Later he tried to think of the "giving" and the "it" such that
the "poietic" (in this sense of "creative") character of a prelogical
occurrence prior to and beyond all thinking becomes visible (cf. below, p. 150), and he tried to do such that from the outset this occurrence will already have gone beyond and encompassed the essence
of man (cf. esp. *ZSD* 20, *19*). The "matter at issue" in giving is expressed in such determinants as "reaching" [*Erreichen*], "donating"
[*Schenken*], as well as the "gift" [*Gabe*] in the sense of the "given
outcome" [*Ergebnis*] of such giving. In particular, this gift was expressed as the open (truth) of a creative "sense of the presence of
the presencing of what is present" that is accessible to recollective
thinking in the first beginning; in a thinking that creatively thinks
ahead to an other beginning it has the "sense" of the "worlding" of
the fourfold and the "thinging" of the things in the experience of
"nearness."

How does Heidegger conceive of the matters at issue in the "it,"
which is not to be taken as a reintroduction of a substance or a
subject? Heidegger characterizes this "it" as the "most inconspicuous of the inconspicuous," as "the simplest of simplicities," as the
"nearest of the near" as well as "the farthest of the far in which we
mortals reside our whole life long" (*UzS* 259, *128*). This is the "relation of all relations," the event of appropriation (ibid., 267, *135*).
The state of affairs in "*es gibt*" is said to be due to the utmost movement of a "granting" (ibid., 258, *127*) in the sense of an "event of
appropriation" that brings each matter or thing in the state of affairs
in "*es gibt*" into what is appropriate to it and maintains it in its belonging together with the others (cf. *ZSD* 20, *19*).

The entire state of affairs in "*es gibt*" is thus other than that in the
traditional concept of the universal and its relationship to the particular. The "*es gibt*" is supposed to be rendered capable of being
experienced in its "prepredicative" structure for those humans who
have already "become mortals" (cf. *VA* 177, *178*), for those who
have been able to wrench themselves from the framework of the

ratio by means of a "leap" (see below, p. 130). Such human beings no longer understand themselves in terms of the *animalitas* of an *animal rationale* (cf. *HBf* 89, 221; *UZS* 173, 70) nor in terms of the idea of death as the impending decay of their bodies. There are two further determinations of what the event of appropriation means for Heidegger that are especially important if we are to think Heidegger further.

The event of appropriation must be viewed in terms of the early Greek *alētheia,* which was conceived of in Heidegger's recollective thinking ahead; it must be seen as a "movement" that in its "sending and extending" still preserves what is most proper to itself, as a movement that holds itself back and "withdraws itself from unrestricted disclosure" (cf. *ZSD* 23, 22). The event of ap-propriation includes an "expropriation" [*Enteignis*] (ibid. and 44, 41). To put it differently, i.e., in terms of the movement of *alētheia:* the event of appropriation is the movement from concealment, the mystery, to disclosure—whereby what is disclosed in each case and what is harbored in the realm of the already unconcealed retain the character of a mystery (cf. above, p. 37).

2. It is the event of appropriation that—until the beginning of our own epoch—granted Being as the presence of what is present. Presence, however, means to be of concern [*Angang*] (ibid., 14–15, 13), so that it can concern the mortals and be accepted by them (cf. ibid., 23, 22).

Does this not imply that for Heidegger it is the event of appropriation that gathers the mortals in their essence such that it reaches out and concerns them—whereby, as we quoted already, "reaching out" [*Be-lang*] is "what reaches out after our essence, issues a demand and thus lets one reach that wherein one belongs" (*UzS* 197, 91). Does this not confirm the assumption that it is the event of appropriation as it reaches out and concerns us that is meant in the quotation cited at the beginning when that which "belongs together with death" is mentioned?

In order to answer this question, we must establish whether or not and, if so, then how, saying on the one hand and death on the other would be conceivable "in terms of the event of appropriation." Let us first turn to saying. It holds without qualification that "the event of appropriation has the character of saying" (ibid., 263,

131). The event of appropriation gathers "the design [*Aufriß*] of saying" (ibid., 259, *128*) and is "what stirs things in the showing [*Zeigen*] of saying" (ibid., 258, *127*). This is "appropriating" [*Eignen*]. For we read: "The appropriating that brings about saying and stirs saying as the showing in its showing is to be called the event of appropriation" (ibid.). "Hearing" the bid or call of saying also belongs to the "appropriating of saying" (cf. ibid., 260, *129*). Heidegger explains: "Making man as the one who hears appropriate for saying is distinguished by the fact that this making-appropriate lets the human essence into what is proper to it, but only so that man, as the one that speaks, i.e., as the sayer, encounters saying, and indeed from out of that which is proper to him." And further: "When mortals are made appropriate for saying, the human essence is let into the usage, out of which man is used, to bring soundless saying into the sounding of language" (ibid.).

The movement of the nearing of the regions' mutual encounter by means of the soundlessly calling gathering, the ringing of stillness, is then determined as "the appropriating event of stillness" (*UzS* 214, *108*).

It is therefore no surprise that Heidegger characterizes saying as the "most proper form of the event of appropriation" (*UzS* 262, *131*) and as the way that the event of appropriation, in speaking, brings "that which is present out of its ownness into shining" (*UzS* 266, *135*). The human essence experiences saying as the "appropriating way" (cf. ibid., 261, *130*) insofar as the essence of language "unfolds its essence" precisely with regard to man, insofar as it "concerns" and "touches" him in the way we have shown.

Did Heidegger conceive of death "in terms of the event of appropriation"? Did he conceive of death as the "mystery of disclosure in its calling"? He certainly did not do so explicitly. But if the event of appropriation for him is in itself "expropriation"—"a word in which the early Greek word '*lēthē*' in the sense of concealment is contained commensurate with the appropriative event" (*ZSD* 44, *40*)—then is not death thought of in terms of the event of appropriation insofar as "the highest concealment of Being" is gathered in death (*UzS* 23, *200*)? In another passage Heidegger then explains that "the essence of mortals is called to attentiveness to the bid that bids them to come toward death" (*VA* 256, *101*). This can only be the bid of the event of appropriation, which calls mortals into that to which they are appropriated. However, as the passage states, as mortals they are appropriated "to the highest shelter (the gathering harboring) of the mystery of disclosure in its calling" (ibid.).

If we now return to the passage from the essay "The Essence of Language" that we took as our starting point, then we can see why the "essential relationship" between death and language can give us "a hint as to the way that the essence of language reaches out and concerns us and thus holds us in relation to it." For it is indeed the case "that death belongs together with that which reaches out and concerns us." Death belongs together with the event of appropriation, to which, as we have shown, saying also belongs. The hint that the essential relationship gives us there lies in the way that the event of appropriation in its saying reaches out and concerns us, calling us "to come to death" as the "highest shelter of the mystery of disclosure in its calling" (*VA* 256, *101*).

Are there then *two* calls that reach one who can hear, or is it *one* call insofar as both of them call into disclosure? The saying that is commensurate with the event of appropriation calls those who hear into the many forms of linguistically articulate disclosure and the concealment that is commensurate with the event of appropriation in its "highest" form as the mystery of death also calls to disclosure in the same way. Do the two calls not sound in unison, i.e., as *one*, so that saying is simply determined through and through by concealedness, the mystery? If this were so, then the way that mortals respond to the address would be fundamentally different from that of those human beings who view their essence in terms of *animalitas* and *ratio*. For the latter, Being has the temporal sense of increasing constancy; the "mortals," however, experience "Being" as the nearing of the play of the world, they experience it out of the mystery-attuned address of the regions of the world. The "poetic dwelling" that would lie in this playing along that is in accord with the address would be determined by the event of appropriation as the essential relationship between death and language. It would be determined no longer by *ratio* or by a "planning, calculating representation" but rather by a conduct guided by a "shyness" that no longer seeks after grounds and principles but has instead experienced itself as harbored in a "groundless" Being.

With the help of Heidegger's basic determinants, we have attempted to conceive of this essential relationship that remained "unthought" by Heidegger himself. Since this attempt is obviously just an outline, the next step would have to be to unfold more exactly the mortals' transformed conduct after it has been attuned by the twofold call. However, this would raise a question that is very urgent for any critical reflection. The question concerns the way that "poetic dwelling" in the age of "an other beginning" is to be understood. What would "everyday praxis" look like? Would there be no further scientific endeavors? Do not all of the possibilities that lie in man's capacity for foundational thinking through understanding also belong to his "essence"? Even if one agrees with Heidegger that man's exclusive understanding of himself in terms of *animalitas* and *ratio* has had grave consequences, one still cannot ignore man's capacity for understanding and for grounding things, for man must bring this capacity into play in his everyday praxis, especially with regard to responsible action in his relationship to his fellow man within a community. Especially if "poetic dwelling" is not supposed to be an "irrational" mood that is opposed to man's "rational" conduct, then thinking would have the task of providing a concrete conception of the very way that those human beings would have to conduct themselves who have become mortals through the essential relationship between death and language.

FIVE

The Measure for
Seinsgeschicklich Thinking

At the end of the "Letter on Humanism" Heidegger asks: "Whence does thinking take its measure? What is the law for what it does?" (*HB* 117, 240).[1] The answer he gives is, "Thinking, in its essence as the thinking of Being, is claimed by Being. . . . Being has already been dispatched to thinking. Being *is* as the *Geschick* of thinking. But this *Geschick* is in itself historical. Its history has already come to language in the saying of the thinkers" (ibid., 117, 240–41).

Let us begin with a very brief sketch of the way that Heidegger's early writings led to this determination of thinking. *Being and Time* described the circular structure in the understanding of something (a being) *as* something (a being). Such understanding is a "thrown projection" of meaning. Beings are "understood" out of the fore-structure of understanding. Concernful Being-in-the-world projects itself toward a totality of significations that has constantly established itself in advance in referential relationships (the worldliness of the world). The inaugural lecture "What Is Metaphysics?" shows that in essential (ontological) anxiety *Dasein* as this Being-in-the-world experiences the "annihilation" of the totality of significations and references and thus of its "world." *Dasein* experiences the world as a Nothing, into which it is "held" as the ground of its *Dasein,* and out of which it cannot ground itself by means of a projection. And through a "return" [*Einkehr*] into *Dasein's* "null ground" or foundation, *Dasein's* fundamental comportment is transformed. Confronted with the experience of its impotence, *Dasein* surmounts the idea of the power of a subject that represents the world to itself as being at its disposal and as being groundable within itself. By contrast, the subject now experiences itself as one whose *Being* has always been grounded in itself. It desists from wanting to ground itself. In this "relinquishment," it becomes clear that the Nothing that *Dasein* encounters in anxiety has the power to "come forth in its essence," since it can rob the "world" of its significance. Thus, Nothing is itself a kind of Being even if, given its provenance, it is merely a "veiled" and "groundless" Being. This Being, which must be experienced as "sending itself" [*zuschickend*] to *Dasein* is as such thought of "historically"—as the *Geschick* that simultaneously manifests itself to and yet withdraws itself from thinking. This thinking is the thinking of the history of Being, the *seinsgeschicklich* thinking that Heidegger attempted to achieve after the "turn." The following quotations from the lecture *Der Satz vom Grund* give a closer illustration of the way he understood "the history of Being" [*Seinsgeschichte*] and "the *Seinsgeschick*." On page 130 we read: "The history of Western thinking rests in the *Geschick* of Being"; on page 108 it is stated that "what is called the *Geschick* of Being characterizes the history of Western thinking until now"; and further on, Heidegger says, "the essence of history is determined by the *Geschick* of Being." When Heidegger speaks of "the history of Being," this expression must therefore be understood in terms of the *Seinsgeschick*. But what does "the *Geschick* of Being" mean, and accordingly, the term "thinking of the history of Being" [*seinsgeschichtliches Denken*] in the sense of "*seinsgeschicklich* thinking?"

Let us first recall the meaning of the word *Geschick,* which goes back to the word *schicken.* The word *schicken* involves three things. First of all, it means "sending" in the sense of bringing or sending something on its way. This can occur with or without grounds; it can be a "groundless" sending in the sense of a "giving whose bestowing is groundless." In the word *schicken* there is also the sense of *sich schicken,* i.e., to be suitable, that which is *schicklich* or "suitable" with regard to something else.

The word *Geschick* especially has the meaning of *Schicksal* or "fate," *fatum;* however, this is not at all the meaning to which Heidegger is referring. For an understanding of the "history of Being and the *Geschick* of Being," the first meaning is the primary one, whereby one should recall that Heidegger uses the German prefix *Ge-* to signify the act of gathering or collecting as well as the having-been-collected of whatever it is one is referring to. Thus the gathering of *"Lauten"* [sounding] is *"Geläut"* [that which sounds]; the gathering of *"Bergen"* [sheltering or harboring] is called *"Gebirg"* [shelter]. The gathering of different ways of *"Schicken"* or sending, the sending that gathers is called *"Geschick"* (cf. *VA* 32, *305–6*).

To what does this "sending that gathers," this *Geschick,* send itself? It sends itself to and in thinking (*HB* 117, *241*); and, as we shall see, it does so as a "giving whose bestowing is groundless." It is just in this regard that it is a *"seinsgeschicklich* thinking," and is such in the broader sense of the word, also, i.e., as that "which is suitable" [*sich schickt*].

The issue here, however, is not *Geschick* or *geschicklich* thinking in general but rather the *Seinsgeschick* and *seinsgeschickliches Denken.* As a further introduction, we might add to these determinations the following remark: it is well known that after the "turn" Heidegger no longer remained a follower of Husserl in inquiring into the "meaning" [*Sinn*] of Being, but that instead he inquired into its "truth." As a matter of course, Being is then taken in a verbal sense as the occurrence of truth, and the latter is taken as the "coming into the clearing" or "self-clearing," as a "disclosing" that came about through a *seinsgeschicklich* thinking that in its disclosure belongs to this occurrence.

Later we shall investigate more closely the way that this occurrence of truth as the occurrence of Being does not coincide for Heidegger with the traditional understanding of the meaning of "truth." It must instead be thought of as *alētheia,* a relationship between concealedness and unconcealedness, between mystery, errancy, and the clearing. Furthermore, since thinking "belongs to" this occurrence of a soundless address, it is capable of listening to it and of giving an articulated response to what it has heard.

The later Heidegger's thinking is usually characterized as *seinsgeschicklich* thinking. However, this general characterization ignores the fact that various directions and intentions within this kind of thinking must be distinguished.

1. There is *seinsgeschicklich* thinking that is oriented toward the fragments of the Presocratics in order to think the truth of the Presocratics' experience with Being at the beginning of Western thinking. This is the truth of Being "in the first beginning." Heidegger's

interpretation of "The Anaximander Fragment" and the essays "Logos" and "Aletheia" serve as examples along these lines.

2. There is *seinsgeschicklich* thinking that is oriented toward the texts of metaphysics such as those of Plato as well as Aristotle, Descartes, Leibniz, Kant, Fichte, Hegel, Schelling, and Nietzsche.

3. There is *seinsgeschicklich* thinking whose concern is "contemplation" [*Besinnung*]. Such contemplation attempts to discover the meaning of the completed form of *Seinsgeschick,* the "meaning" of the "essential unfolding of technology" today. It attempts to discover the "truth of an other beginning," of the "turning in Being" for which such contemplation prepares the way. Examples here are "The Question Concerning Technology" and "The Turn."

4. There is a *seinsgeschicklich* thinking that sees its primary task in the "preparation" of an "other" beginning in thinking and experiencing as opposed to the first beginning of the Presocratics. This is a *seinsgeschicklich* thinking that, in its enactment of the "turning of Being," transforms itself into a "saying of Being." Examples here are "The Thing" and "Building, Dwelling, Thinking." [2]

In spite of these differences, what is common to all four of these directions in *seinsgeschicklich* thinking is that they are all interpretations, modes of a hermeneutics. But what kind of a hermeneutics? It certainly is not a traditional hermeneutics in the sense of a theory of art. Nor is it, as in *Being and Time,* the articulation of the self-understanding of understanding *Dasein* in the circumspection that takes place in the mode of everydayness, a prepredicative projective understanding of Being that is prestructured by facticity and thrownness. It is not concerned with the mode of Being that distinguishes *Dasein,* i.e., the "understanding of Being"—of Being proper and the Being of its Being-in-the-world. Here we no longer have the circular structure of understanding and the interpretive understanding in which one must still distinguish between fore-having, fore-sight, and fore-conception. The concern in Heidegger's later interpretations is different from the conception of hermeneutics and interpretation in *Being and Time,* and it is different from the conceptions of hermeneutics that have taken as a point of orientation the conception of "understanding" developed there.

As the thesis of this chapter, I shall attempt to show that Heidegger's sole concern in his interpretation of the Presocratic fragments was to express in "the words of Being" a particular meaning of Being in the first beginning, a meaning that served as an unthematized measure and guided his entire *seinsgeschicklich* thinking. Furthermore, in his interpretation—guided as it was by this measure—of the traditional texts of metaphysics, Heidegger's sole concern was to make evident the "words of withdrawal" of this meaning of Being so that these words could, in "an other saying of Being," be transformed into "words of Being" (cf. *SvG* 205ff.) for "preparatory thinking." This latter meaning is the one that in any case guided Heidegger's "contemplation" of "that which is today."

It might seem strange that this should be the only goal of *seinsgeschicklich* thinking. And it might seem even stranger that now "out of the truth of Being thinking transforms itself to an other saying" (ibid., 159). This implies that *seinsgeschicklich* thinking is such that it is in the process of and has accomplished a transformation out of the traditional ways of thinking. In order to clarify the structure of this thinking, then, the first question is, how does such a transformation occur and in what does it consist? The first section of this chapter is an attempt to answer this question.

Since the transformation is supposed to follow "from the truth of Being," we will then ask in the second section what "the truth of Being" means in this context. Is this determinant perhaps related to the measure that Heidegger himself did not thematize? The third section will then attempt to clarify the purpose and goal of *seinsgeschicklich* thinking.

I

How does the transformation of thinking occur? Heidegger has called this transformation a "leaping."[3] What structures are contained in the idea of "leaping"?

1. "Leaping" means, among other things, that this *seinsgeschicklich* thinking, which is other than traditional thinking, requires no philosophical propaedeutic such as the "Phenomenology of Spirit" was for Hegel's "Logic" in the *Encyclopedia* or the way that "negative philosophy" was a necessary propaedeutic for Schelling's positive, free thinking.

2. "Leaping" means "to leap away from" all deductive or dia-

lectical conceptual thought, all sorts of "foundationalist" thinking. Since the various sorts of traditional thinking had a common
method in the step-by-step progression toward their goals, "leaping" means that this method has been abandoned in favor of a
thinking that is accomplished without the steadiness of a progression. This does not mean that the thinking that is in the process of
transforming itself or has completed this process stands in no relation to the realm from which it has departed. *Seinsgeschicklich*
thinking, especially the first two directions we listed, does after all
direct itself to traditional texts; it thus maintains a particular relationship to the tradition. Such "leaping away" does, however,
mean that this relationship to the tradition is transformed, which is
why the text shows itself in a novel way.

3. Whoever wishes to leap away must prepare for his leap. Whoever wishes to leap away from "foundationalist" thinking must remind himself that and how all prephilosophical representation of
things is determined by a search for grounds such that all beings
appear to it as capable of being explained and grounded. That is
why one must come to the clear insight that metaphysical thinking
took all beings to be capable of being explained and grounded in
the form of a judgment. In the third section we will show how
Leibniz's metaphysical thinking articulated just this view in the
"principle of sufficient reason."

After this "preparation," *seinsgeschicklich* thinking finds itself "in
the leap." From the new posture of "Being-in-the-leap," it is able to
look back at the area from which it leapt. Only from this vantage
point can it catch sight of what it could not see hitherto. This is,
first of all, metaphysics as a whole and the determinations that
govern it as such. Furthermore, *seinsgeschicklich* thinking, by being
"in-the-leap," can see that the whole of metaphysics has manifested itself in various ways to foundationalist thinking, and as
we have shown for Heidegger, in various forms or dispatchings
[*Zu-schickungen*] or *Geschicke*. Heidegger writes: "We cannot conceive of that which is called the *Geschick* of Being as long as we
have not performed the leap" (*SvG* 108).

Thinking directed to the whole of metaphysics and its various
Geschicke is especially the theme of the second kind of *seinsgeschicklich* thinking that was mentioned above, i.e., thinking that is

directed to the traditional texts of metaphysics. We will later show which connection it has to the other forms of *seinsgeschicklich* thinking.

4. "Being-in-the-leap" also signifies something else with regard to the character of *seinsgeschicklich* thinking that is in the process of or has completed a self-transformation, although this is something that Heidegger himself did not make clear. Whoever has leaped away and is in-the-leap is not attuned in the same way as is one who remains in the foundationalist posture, either in his everyday nonscientific conduct or in his philosophizing. In order to understand what *seinsgeschicklich* thinking is, it is essential to note that leaping away entails an abandonment of these kinds of attunement. This is ultimately the case because it involves the abandonment of the familiar and seemingly secure region upon which all foundationalist thinking is based as though upon an unshakable foundation; it is the abandonment of the region based upon *ratio* understood in this sense as "ground." Only non-everyday, nonscientific ways of thinking, only a philosophizing that does not ground things in the traditional way can find itself moved by that which would never be of "concern" to it otherwise. The attunement of a scholar or scientist, say, a historian who presents the material available to him from the standpoint of historical objectivity, is precisely not that of *seinsgeschicklich* thinking which finds itself in the posture of "being-in-the-leap." It is only in the attunement of *seinsgeschicklich* thinking that our tradition "comes to be present" [*anwest*], to use Heidegger's term; only for this attunement is there that which "comes to have been" [*Gewesendes*]. And it is only "that which comes to have been" and is as such "thought back upon" that *seinsgeschicklich* thinking is supposed to "appropriate anew," is supposed to recollectively think ahead. In the literature on Heidegger, a "recollective thinking ahead" has been frequently spoken of, but it has been frequently overlooked that such thinking requires an other attunement. The only thinking that can be properly so called is the "renewed appropriation of what comes to have been" [*Neu-Aneignen vom Gewesenden*], the renewed appropriation of a *Geschick* that comes to have been.

5. Leaping as "renewed appropriation" means that *seinsgeschicklich* thinking, as recollective leaping, is also at the same time a "leap

forward." It is a thinking ahead that can develop further into the preparatory thinking we mentioned as the fourth direction. Into which realm does *seinsgeschicklich* thinking leap forward? It leaps into "the realm of that which first arrives as something worthy of thought (cf. *SvG* 150ff.). However, if this arrival is also influenced by the traits of what has been and can only be recognized in them, then recollective thinking's "that which has been" must contain "what is yet unthought as that which is to be thought" (ibid., 158). This is what thinking responds to insofar as it is recollective and anticipatory. But what is worthy of recollective thinking ahead? Heidegger's answer is "the truth of Being."

I quoted the passage in which Heidegger demands that "from the truth of Being, thinking must transform itself into an other saying of Being" (ibid., 159). Until now we have seen only that this transformation is the "leaping of a leap" and that this is the only way that thought can attain a recollective thinking of what has been; and that, at the same time, this is a thinking ahead of what is to be thought, of what is yet unthought and worthy of thought. One might add to these determinations of recollective thinking ahead that for Heidegger such thinking involves "beholding what is audible," in particular "what was previously un-heard" (ibid., 86). These paradoxical-sounding characterizations do not refer to physiological hearing with one's ears or seeing with one's eyes. This "hearing" [*Hören*] is only possible through a "belonging" [*Zugehören*], a belonging to the "truth of Being" into which man's essence ek-statically stands out (cf. *HB* 69ff., 205ff.). For, as Heidegger states, man's essence "belongs" to Being, it is "thrown by Being into the preservation of its truth [*Wahrnis seiner Wahrheit*] and laid claim to for its sake" (ibid., 111, 237). Heidegger never said so, but I am convinced of the following: interpretive *seinsgeschicklich* thinking has, by means of the posture of "being-in-the-leap," already been transformed into a "beholding hearing." This is so because it has experienced itself as belonging to the truth of Being, it keeps its eyes and ears trained on just this—the truth of Being—in its interpretation of the text. Since Heidegger's view of the "essence of language" was also other than the traditional one, he could put it this way, too: such thinking holds itself in "the soundless address of the truth of Being" which is based upon a very definitive "meaning," a meaning that, according to the central thesis of this essay, implicitly governs all *seinsgeschicklich* thinking as its measure.

Now, those who recall Heidegger's own reflections in his various interpretations of metaphysical texts may object, saying that he conceived of this interpretation as a "dialogue" with the tradition, so that the "truth of Being" or even a measure is spoken of only peripherally or not at all. We shall deal with the structure of this "dialogue" later. First, however, we should show what Heidegger's determination "the truth of Being" means and wherein its character as a measure lies.

II

The determination "the truth of Being" is central to Heidegger's later thinking. Though it designates an issue that has a number of aspects, we shall direct our attention to only a few of them in the present context.[4] The term "truth" means approximately the same thing after the "turn" as what in *Being and Time* was called "meaning" [*Sinn*] with regard to understanding as a projection (cf. 151ff., 230; cf. also *HBf* 84, *217*). Furthermore, "truth" is supposed to refer to the issue that, according to Heidegger's interpretation, was denoted by the early Greek determination of *alētheia*.[5] Initially he laid out this determination in the lecture "On the Essence of Truth." It refers to the occurrence of making something manifest, of a lighting up; it refers to the establishment of a clearing, a disclosure of the *lēthē* that belongs to *a-lētheia,* where *lēthē* reigns as the "concealing of the concealedness of beings as a whole, and that is of Being" (*WdW* 20, *135;* 25, *139*). As "mystery" and as the "refusing and dissembling" (*Hw* 42, *54*) "errancy" (*WdW* 20–21, *135–36*), the *lēthē* permeates all disclosure in a number of ways. The first of these is by harboring what is concealed as that which is to be disclosed; it releases that which is to be disclosed as the *Geschick* that is current at the time into disclosure such that *lēthē* continues to hold sway over this "unconcealedness" and what is unconcealed therein. Another way is that concealment completely withdraws what is concealed within itself and only discloses itself as withdrawal, or even conceals itself as such so that this entire occurrence of truth as such is "forgotten."

This was just what had increasingly occurred during the pre-dominance of metaphysics, according to Heidegger (cf. *ZSD* 78, 71). "Metaphysics" is not just one discipline in academic philoso-phy for him, but rather rules in all areas that are related to the whole of beings. It has a decisive influence on whatever is taken as nature, culture, politics, ideals, and ideologies and as the nature of man, his plans, representations of things, or his calculations—in short, whatever is "real."

This *Geschick* showed itself in various forms that led to a "forgot-tenness of Being as the occurrence of truth." It especially shows it-self, however, as the "claim" on or "address" to thinking to which the philosophers of metaphysics responded without any insight into the sense in which the *Geschick* was an occurrence of truth de-termined by this withdrawal.

What consequences for a determination of *seinsgeschicklich* think-ing follow from the above-mentioned aspects of the issue that forms the basis for Heidegger's discussion of "the truth of Being"? Insofar as such thinking is directed toward interpreting meta-physical texts, it is an established fact for it that these texts are evi-dence for a "withdrawal" that extended up to a total forgottenness of the occurrence of truth.

What is important here is to note clearly just what has really been withdrawn by this *seinsgeschicklich* development. What with-draws itself here did not withdraw itself in the *Geschick* of the first beginning to which the Presocratics responded. Nor does it with-draw itself in the *Geschick* thought of in an other beginning, in the "truth of Being" as it is preparatorily thought of in thinking ahead. What withdraws itself from the *Geschicke* of metaphysics is the meaning, the "measure" that Heidegger gained through his *seinsge-schicklich* interpretations of the Presocratic texts and his "dialogue" with Hölderlin. It is a measure that he himself did not thematize, however.[6] With reference to the meaning of *poiēsis,* we may call this measure the "poietic." This is the meaning that Hölderlin's words "poetically man dwells" had for Heidegger. It is the same meaning that is supposed to make up man's "dwelling in another beginning" (cf. below, pp. 147–57). Our thesis is that this measure determines the "content" of "the truth of Being" and is what *seinsgeschicklich* thinking has its "gaze" (or its ear) directed to whenever it interprets traditional metaphysical texts. This measure is what *seinsgeschicklich* thinking expresses in "words of Being." It is when the *Geschicke* of metaphysics are measured according to this measure in a true sense that they are seen as ways of "withdrawal"—which is what the second kind of thinking that we mentioned above expressed in "words of withdrawal."

In *Being and Time,* the early Heidegger employed such determinants as "Being-ready-to-hand" and "authenticity" in order to overcome the Cartesian "ontology of Being-present-at-hand." The later Heidegger achieved something similar by means of the "words of Being" that together constitute the content of the "truth" of Being in the first beginning.

The most important "words of Being" should be named in order to illustrate the "poietic" character underlying them.[7] The later Heidegger's *seinsgeschicklich* recollective thinking ahead is a confirmation of his early insight in "On the Essence of Reasons," whereby the "unveiledness of Being" makes possible the "manifestness of beings" for *Dasein* in its understanding of Being (*SuZ* 13–14). The grammatical form of *eon* in Anaximander's and Parmenides' thinking testifies to the unity of an original duality in the Being of beings: the unity of an occurrence of Being, which is to be conceived of verbally, and of beings that are to be thought of in a nominal sense. The recollective thinking ahead in "The Anaximander Fragment" discloses the internal mobility of the *eon* in the very way that the *eon* of the *eonta* realizes itself ever anew as difference. This internal mobility has the character of a "poietic" vitality that shows itself especially in the temporal character of *eon*. For *seinsgeschicklich* interpretation, this character was involved in the sudden occurrence of an emergence into the "jointure" [*Fuge*] of a "lingering" and in the just as sudden disappearance out of it. The temporal sense of this "lingering" was determined as the state of presence [*Gegenwart*] of an "abrupt" [*jäher*] nature. In order to make it possible in the German language to experience the temporal sense of the occurrence of Being "as it is thought in Greek," Heidegger translated the *eon* into "*Anwesen*" [coming-to-presence] or "*anwesend*" [presencing] and *eonta* into "*Anwesende*" [that which is present]. These words all contain the sense of an original state of presence. In the "abruptness" of the state of presence, one can per-

ceive the "poietic" character of the occurrence of coming to presence in the first beginning. Then one can also recognize why for
Heidegger it was the withdrawal of this character that led coming
to presence [*Anwesen*] in the temporal meaning of the state of being
present [*Gegenwart*] to become ever more "persistent" and thus
"noncreative" in the subsequent epochs of metaphysics.

The "poietic" character of Being in the first beginning shows itself especially well, however, in the meaning of the "word of Being"
physis. *Physis* is the power to pro-duce something on its own, to
bring forth and step out into the light, a stepping out that is at the
same time a stepping away into the realm of concealedness.

My conviction, according to which the meaning of Being in the
first beginning had a "poietic" character, is also especially confirmed by the meaning of the "word of Being" *logos*. Heidegger's interpretation discovers the sense of a gathering-collecting power
there, a power that rekindles ever anew a "primordial strife" in
Being and seeks to reconcile this strife by means of a "groundless
grounding." Here he discovers a power that reigns for its own sake
and not for the sake of man, who demands grounds and principles
for beings. This should suffice as an illustration of the meaning of
the poietic character of the contents in the "words of Being" in the
first beginning and the meaning of this measure.

In order to achieve an understanding of *seinsgeschicklich* thinking
that interprets the texts of metaphysics, it is therefore of great importance to note that this thinking is concerned with the *Geschicke*
of an all-encompassing poietic sense of Being in the first beginning
that subsequently withdraws itself. That is the very reason why
the interpretation simply assumes that these texts are not concerned with "words of Being." As a result of the interpretation, one
will instead be able to find "words of the withdrawal of the poietic
meaning of Being in the first beginning," words of withdrawal that
will be different according to the particular "epochs" reigning in
metaphysics. One such word is, for example, "subjectity," the essential unfolding of the subject's subjectivity that we find as the
result of Heidegger's interpretation of the introduction to Hegel's
Phenomenology of Spirit. Another is the "will to will," which can
be seen as a result of the interpretations of Nietzsche (*Hw* 218,
79–80). These "words of withdrawal" are what now in turn set

thinking on the way to a truth of Being "in another beginning." This is the path upon which Heidegger embarked by following the structure of *seinsgeschicklich* thinking. He thus applied "thinking ahead" both in his interpretations of the Presocratic fragments we mentioned under the first heading and in his recollective thinking mentioned as the second kind of *seinsgeschicklich* thinking. He then proceeded to take the determinations he gained in thinking ahead and transformed them into a "saying of Being" by means of the "preparatory" thinking mentioned under the fourth heading. The leading consideration, however, continued to be the "measure" that lay in the all-encompassing poietic sense of the "truth of Being" in the first beginning, which—as we should explicitly note here—had been gained in the thinker's dialogue with poetry, especially with that of Hölderin. Thus, e.g., in preparatory thinking, Heidegger conceived of the meaning of *eon* as an "*es gibt*" ["there is" or "it gives"] and developed its meaning in various determinations such as "bestowing," "presenting," etc. One example of this is the presentation of "time" and "space" in the granting enspacing and temporalizing of a "time-play-space" [*Zeitspielraum*] for the appearance of whatever is present. Above all, his thinking ahead proceeded from this vantage point to conceive of the determinants "the event of appropriation" and "appropriating" as the guiding words for his preparatory thinking. These determinants thereby characterize the occurrence that brings each thing into what is proper to it, an occurrence that was capable of being grasped neither by a "universal concept" nor by the "concept" [*Begriff*] in Hegel's sense.

III

In order to answer this chapter's third main question, the question of what the purpose and goal of *seinsgeschicklich* thinking is, the determinant "appropriating" is of special significance. We have shown that "beholding hearing" with regard to the address of the "truth of Being" is grounded in the fact that it "belongs to" "the truth of Being." The determinant "appropriating" expresses this "belonging" in an even more essential manner by seeing "thinking" as completely "expropriated" to the "truth of Being" and by seeing that this constitutes "what is proper" to the human essence. In this light, one can thus understand what it meant for Heidegger that Being determines "man as he who ek-sists, to guardianship over the truth of Being" (*HBf 95, 224*). The various kinds of thinking we have distinguished therefore actually all serve to prepare a meaning of Being that is commensurate with an other beginning.

Heidegger himself called the interpretation of a traditional text a "dialogue," a "conversation within the tradition and with it." As he stated in his lecture course "What Is Called Thinking?," the interpreter is supposed to "have previously entered into what has been said, into the issue that is expressed in language there" (108, *174*). In the lecture "The Anaximander Fragment," he requires that the interpreter, "listening, enter into that which comes to language in the saying" (*Hw* 306, *22*). Is this "listening to" identical with that "beholding hearing" of that address of the truth of Being that we have spoken of up until now? This is not the case. Above all, the listening simply concerns the address of language that gives a hint "to us first and then again in the end as to the essence of the matter at issue" (*VA* 190, *216*). The interpreter must follow the "hints" of language and bring what was previously covered up and unsaid, "the unapparent," to appearance. To this extent, one could say that the entry into *seinsgeschicklich* thinking is still "phenomenological" since it uncovers the "essence" that it has beheld with its essential view, so that the provenance of this essence becomes apparent and this essence is brought to language.

The matter at issue in a text presents itself to the interpreter in the form of language. Language addresses the tradition to him in its ambiguous way. The interpreter then understands what is addressed to him in and through his language, i.e., from the particular understanding of the world that is sedimented in his language, just as he understands the matter at issue in terms of those presuppositions in his thinking that for the most part are not transparent to him.

It is in accord with the meaning of a "dialogue" that, as Heidegger demands, the interpreter is not only supposed to deal with the matter at issue in the text, but that he also "must contribute something of his own to this issue without insisting upon it" (*Hw* 197,

58). Thus Heidegger notes in "The Anaximander Fragment" that "one can speak of the same thing from different points of view" (ibid., 307, 23).

In these and several other determinations, Heidegger does not seem to differ from other views in contemporary philosophy concerning the essence of an interpretation. However, further on in the same passage, Heidegger states in connection with the term "sameness" that "this is that same thing that as a *Geschick* concerns the Greeks and us in different ways" (ibid., 310, 24). Here it becomes clear that *seinsgeschicklich* interpretation deals on with *Geschicke,* with *Geschicke* of Being; but, particularly in metaphysical thinking, these *Geschicke* have manifested themselves only in the form of the withdrawal of the creative meaning of Being in the first beginning. That is why, as we have shown, Heidegger assumes in his interpretation of metaphysical texts that a given text is evidence of the self-withdrawing meaning of creative Being. That is precisely the reason why he sees his task in bringing into view that this *Geschick* is just such a withdrawal in one or another and how it is so. For instance, in his presentation of Leibniz's metaphysical thinking, he simply assumes that Leibniz's thinking was such a form of withdrawal; the task then is to show how it was subject to the claim of the *Geschick* of self-withdrawing Being. One of the consequences that follows from this sense of withdrawal is the following, as we mentioned: metaphysical thinking, in having "forgotten" that the occurrence of Being is an occurrence of truth, constructed "guiding projections" from a restricted viewpoint and employed them to represent beings as such in its attempt to determine their essence. Accordingly, the guiding projection in Leibniz's metaphysical thinking was represented by the modern conception of "*ratio*" as ground. It was in light of this *ratio* that all beings appeared to him as grounded and groundable. It was in light of this projection that Leibniz declared, "No being is without a rational ground"—*nihil est sine ratione.* Leibniz's thought was furthermore so determined by the guiding projection of *ratio* that he held it to be a "principle" which requires that the ground must be referred back and conveyed to the representing I in the form of a sufficient truth in judgment. This is what is stated in the *principium reddendae rationis sufficientis,* under whose claim thinking had become rational in the sense of "giving an account" or "justification." The task of *seinsgeschicklich* thinking thus consists in interpreting these determinations of Leibniz as evidence of the withdrawal of the all-encompassing creative meaning of Being and thereby to make visible the historical effects that the "principle of conveying grounds to human understanding" had on modern philosophy and science.

As far as modern philosophy is concerned, *seinsgeschicklich* thinking disclosed how Kant was still subject to the claim of the *Geschick* as Leibniz was. It shows the direction and realm of Kant's inquiry into the conditions for the possibility of nature and freedom were likewise determined by the guiding projection of *ratio,* and even more clearly in light of the twofold sense of *ratio* reason [*Vernunft*] and ground [*Grund*]. *Seinsgeschicklich* thinking discloses that in Kant's inquiries the dimension of the "I-ness" of the "I," the subjectivity of the subject, emerged as the genuine realm for the projection of *ratio.* This realm is transcendental consciousness, which as ground allows the objectivity of objects to be conveyed to it such that it thereby also represents itself as self-consciousness.

We need not pursue further how subjectivity is developed for the subjectivity of reason, for *ratio* as determined by the *principium rationis,* nor do we need to pursue how *seinsgeschicklich* thinking sees the development of objectivity as the *Geschick* of the self-withdrawal of Being in its creative sense. Nor can we pursue how the Leibnizean determinations that bear on modern science disclosed the claim to power that was inherent within these determinations, the claim of *ratio* to be a universal and complete account of everything so that everything becomes calculable—with the result that our age has become the "atomic age."

In line with the interpretation we have described, *seinsgeschicklich* thinking found the "word of withdrawal" of the creative sense of being in the determination of *ratio.* As such it could have stopped there. However, it also proceeds retrospectively. Once again proceeding from the guiding projection that Leibniz employed to conceive of beings as groundable and explainable, *seinsgeschicklich* thinking returns as an "exposition" [*Erörterung*] back to the site or sphere [*Ort*] from which *logos* had emerged as a ground that grounds for its own sake. One then comes to see in what way the determination of *logos* as the grounding ground belongs to the determination of

Being as "the same." But if "Being" and "ground" are "the same," then that implies that Being reigns as ground; and since it is therefore not grounded in any ground, it is as such groundless.

In the lecture course *Der Satz vom Grund,* Heidegger had already employed thinking ahead to think of this groundless Being as a playing. By means of "preparatory thinking" in the lectures "The Thing" and "Building, Dwelling, Thinking," he then developed it further as the "play of the world regions," as a playing in which man's essential Being, as one of those regions, finds its abode in a "responding which, being in the essence of the world and addressed by it, answers that appeal within it" (*VA* 180, *181–82*). An exposition of this determination would go beyond the scope of this essay, but it is still important to point out how the preparatory thinking we arranged under the fourth heading develops out of a further transformation of thinking that itself has been transformed into recollective thinking ahead. At the outset, I quoted the passage from the lecture course *Der Satz vom Grund* in which Heidegger demands that thinking must be transformed "from the truth of Being" into a "saying of Being." The final transformation of thinking, however, can be attained only by means of a "real leap," a "*Satz*"[8] in the sense of a jump. Thus thinking that has already been transformed still undertakes this "leap," this "jump." The "beholding hearing" is thereby also further transformed and listens to Leibniz's principle of reason "in an other key." In contrast to the usual key, in which this principle is heard as "*Nothing* is *without* ground," it is now heard as "Nothing *is* without *ground*." The emphasis has shifted from the "Nothing" to "is" and from "without" to "ground." This shift in key allows such transformed thinking to hear a connection between "is," i.e., "Being," and the "ground." The new key in *Der Satz vom Grund* states that "something like ground belongs to Being"; and this belonging, as we have said, means that Being itself is grounding in the form of a groundless occurrence.

This example of a particularly radical form of *seinsgeschicklich* thinking dealing with traditional metaphysical texts was cited here to illustrate how Heidegger's interpretation of traditional texts simply moves away from them. One must keep in mind that, because of its very meaning, thinking "belongs" to the truth of Being for Heidegger and that he took seriously the mission of a "guardianship" over the "truth of Being" that results from this belonging. For only then can one sanction the violence of such *seinsgeschicklich* interpretations. Only then can one understand why Heidegger considered himself justified in simply thinking things that are unsaid, yet unthought, or even unheard of, into the text and how in the present example he could advocate hearing things in a new key.

It is obvious that it would be futile for a critique of the later Heidegger's interpretations to examine whether or not this or that Heideggerian conclusion is "correct." Heidegger would presumably have granted their "incorrectness" without any further ado, for, as we have seen, he had a completely different concern. We have recognized that the tradition was merely a "springboard" for him. A critique would therefore be meaningful only if it served to prepare for a genuine "thinking further," i.e., only if it is pointed to inconsistencies or deficiencies within the entire conception of his *seinsgeschicklich* thinking, or by rendering insofar as possible this thinking questionable from an external standpoint, for instance in view of the question whether or not and in which sense its goal is "utopian."

One could argue whether or not Kant's or Hegel's thinking was still subject to the *Geschick* that is supposed to have found its most definitive expression in Leibniz; one might doubt that all forms of "metaphysical" thinking are without qualification "forms of the withdrawal of the truth of Being in the first beginning"; but that would still not be a fundamental refutation of the entire conception of his *seinsgeschicklich* thinking.

To avoid misunderstanding it should finally be emphasized that, particularly for *seinsgeschicklich* thinking, which has in view of the "truth of Being" that reigns today, i.e., in view of the essential unfolding of technology, mankind must think "foundationalistically," indeed, in a calculating, representational manner. One could, however, inquire further into this "must," this necessity, in an immanent criticism, for it was possible for Heidegger's own thinking to become *seinsgeschicklich,* and hence for it to free itself from the claim of the *Geschick* reigning today. Heidegger himself even mentioned the possibility of such "freedom" in *Der Satz vom Grund.*

There he says, "The leap remains a free possibility for thinking, so decisively, that the essential realm of freedom even opens itself only within the realm of the leap" (357).

Why did Heidegger not provide anything more than such brief hints? This question is especially pressing in view of the fact that from the time of his work "On the Essence of Truth" onwards, he allowed the essence of freedom to become absorbed in the essence of truth (cf. above, p. 34). Since he even conceived of the essence of truth as the "unconcealedness" that lacks any measure at all, one cannot avoid the impression that Heidegger was perhaps never truly struck by "the wonder of freedom."

Finally, by way of conclusion, we must still answer the question whether or not and in which sense *seinsgeschicklich* thinking that deals with metaphysical texts can be characterized as a "hermeneutics" that is in a certain sense even "speculative."

It is well known that Heidegger himself explicitly declared that his later thinking was not hermeneutical. However, in connection with his attempt to conceive of the essence of language in a manner completely other than that of the tradition, Heidegger remarked that language in its silent saying, the address understood as a non-human event, involves the relationship of a "message" to a "messenger." Hermes was the messenger who received a message and passed it on. Accordingly, Heidegger speaks of a "hermeneutic relationship" that is involved in saying. It was the thesis of this chapter that *seinsgeschicklich* thinking listens for the soundless address of the truth of Being, the all-encompassing meaning creatively established in the first beginning, whenever it interprets a metaphysical texts as a particular *Geschick* of the poietic meaning of Being that withdraws itself. According to my opinion *seinsgeschicklich* thinking acts as a messenger in keeping this message "in mind"; and that is precisely the reason why it is able to interpret the text as more than just a "withdrawal of Being." That is why it can instead transform itself into an "other saying of Being." It therefore does not seem to be inappropriate to characterize Heidegger's *seinsgeschicklich* thinking as a "hermeneutics"—a hermeneutics, however, that is different from the usual ways of interpretive understanding in that, in its attention to the text, it hears and conveys a message that no one has ever heard before.

But in what sense can it be seen as a "speculative" hermeneutics? The thesis of this essay has been that *seinsgeschicklich* thinking interprets the text in terms of the address of the poietic sense of Being. This implies that it is by no means a freely projecting thinking. If the address to thinking did not occur, then there would be "no word of Being" from the Presocratics' fragments, and no "word of withdrawal of the creative sense of Being" would emerge from the texts of metaphysics.

In his doctrine of the "speculative sentence," Hegel demonstrated how the conceptualizing concept itself emerges as the "subject" in a dialectical movement of its determinations. This self-movement of the concept is an event that occurs for that conceptualizing thinking that realizes itself as concept. Hegel calls this occurrence of the concept's self-movement "speculative." Perhaps one can, in an analogous fashion, also call "speculative" that which, out of the address of the truth of Being, happens to *seinsgeschicklich* thinking, i.e., the fact that for such thinking "words of the withdrawal of Being" or "words of Being" emerge from the traditional texts.

Hegel also demonstrated that the usual form of judgment does not suffice for a "presentation" of this speculative movement of the concept. This speculative "presentation" requires a possibility for expression that is other than the usual form of judgments. Likewise, Heidegger's expositions often cannot be expressed in the usual form of a statement, above all because in everyday language "is" serves as a copula and is thus a means of connecting particular beings. By contrast, that which the transformed *seinsgeschicklich* thinking beholdingly hears in the other kind of attunement of being-in-the-leap cannot be easily expressed in the language of judgments. For, according to the metaphysical conception of the construction of beings, the language of judgments attributes the predicates, the *symbebēkota,* to the subject, the *hypokeimenon.* Perhaps one could analogously call the *seinsgeschicklich* presentation "speculative" on account of the relationship between *seinsgeschicklich* thinking and speaking on the one hand and the everyday form of judgments on the other. I would therefore answer the question of whether or not *seinsgeschicklich* thinking is a speculative hermeneutics with a qualified yes.

In its own way, this qualification reminds us of Heidegger's answer to the question, "Whence does thinking take its measure? What is the law for what it does?" The answer is: "The only matter at issue in thinking" is "to bring to language again and again the arrival of Being that remains, and in its remaining awaits man" (*HBf* 118, *241*). Whenever thinking, as historically recollective, heeds the *Geschick* of Being, it has already bound itself to what is fitting, whatever fits in with what is sent to it [*das Schickliche*]. For Heidegger, the measure thought of as the first "law of thinking" is not logic, for logic could become a rule for thinking only on the basis of a law of Being. The measure is rather the "fittingness of saying." Such thinking must gather language into the simply saying; it must lay inconspicuous furrows in language with its saying. This is the descent of thinking and its determination as "absolute knowledge" into what Hegel has called "the poverty of its provisional essence."

SIX

The Measure for Poetry

I

All of Heidegger's later works seek to prepare for the possibility of an other beginning of creative human Being—"other" as compared to the "first beginning" that was brought about by the poetic philosophizing of the Presocratics. For Heidegger, the necessity of such a new beginning follows from his insight into the "supreme danger" that lies in the essential unfolding of technology. This essential unfolding threatens to lead to a state of affairs in which man, in a completely uncreative manner, produces nothing but *"Bestand"* and is no longer capable of viewing his own essence as anything but *"Bestand."* The advent of an other beginning would be, in Hölderlin's words, *"das Rettende,"* i.e., that which would save us. It would be a kind of dwelling that, with reference to Hölderlin, is called "poetic": "poetically, man dwells on this earth. . . ."

Whatever the precise meaning of such "poetic dwelling" may be, Heidegger sees in "poetic dwelling" the possibility of a primordial and hale abiding of man on this planet. Heidegger's thinking is meant to help prepare the way for the realization of this possibility. In the recent history of thought and especially in the history of philosophy, there have, of course, been numerous examples of efforts to save mankind by bringing about a primordial, hale state of affairs.[1] However, it is precisely when one tries to situate Heidegger's later works within the general tendencies of our time that what is unique in his efforts becomes apparent, for in Heidegger's thinking such a primordial state is supposed to take on the form of man's "poetic" dwelling. But what does "poetic" mean? One can, in any case, infer from this determination that the poet and poetry play a decisive role in bringing about the other beginning, regardless of how the task of the philosopher, the thinker, may be conceived of in relation to it.

The purpose of this chapter is, in the first place, to clarify the presuppositions that made it possible for Heidegger to arrive at the view that the poet and poetry play this unusual, even extraordinary role. In the second place, we shall inquire into whether or not it is at all conceivable that the poet's acceptance and realization of this role can lead to "poetic dwelling" for him who is not a "poet," or more precisely, for humanity in general; and we shall also inquire into how this is concretely possible.

I am of course aware that this attempt to direct a question to Heidegger—phrased in terms of his "efforts" toward "goals" and of the poet's "role," which if assumed and realized is supposed to "lead to something"—is open to objection. One could object that, in the first place, it does not take into account that the advent of the "other beginning" for Heidegger occurs "abruptly." Hence its advent cannot be a "goal" that one could "make an effort" to achieve. Second, one could object that this kind of question is contrary to Heidegger's way of thinking as well as to the meaning of the basic determinants he developed.

My reply to the first objection is that in the following I am dealing only with the conditions that must already have been fulfilled before the abrupt advent of the other beginning can occur. This is precisely how Heidegger himself proceeds. I will have to grant the second objection, however. I do indeed intend to proceed immanently in my criticism, but this itself means that I intend to examine Heidegger's "whole project" with regard to the question of whether or not Heidegger's thoughts are consistent and have been thought through to the end. Thus I feel justified in employing an approach that seems to me to be the only one suitable for this purpose.

II

In the following pages I do not intend to depict the development of Heidegger's thought. Nevertheless, I would like to characterize briefly the transformation that his thinking must already have undergone in order to arrive at the dimension within which his thinking took on the task of determining the "possibilities" that could lead to an other beginning of "poetic dwelling." This dimension presents us with the first of the presuppositions in his thinking that enabled him to attribute a special role to the poet.

First of all, Heidegger must already have realized that the determination of *Dasein*'s fundamental structure, its "transcendence" taken as Being-in-the-world, is inappropriate because of the direction in which it moves. Transcendence occurs as an opening of oneself to an interrelated totality of meanings, to the world; *Dasein* proceeds beyond "beings as a whole" to the world as the "upon which" [*Woraufhin*] ("Vom Wesen des Grundes," 20–21; *SuZ* 87). The "understanding of Being" moves in the same "direction." Though thrown, *Dasein* projects itself toward the meaning of Being and the ways of various beings' Being, for instance toward readiness-to-hand and presence-at-hand. By contrast, Heidegger must eventually have become aware that it is first and foremost the world and Being that "give" or "grant" to *Dasein* that entities that are present appear in their presence, and how they do so. At this point the event of "appropriation" [*Ereignis*] or "appropriating" [*Ereignen*] especially characterizes this altered sense of direction for him. It is what expresses the "giving" or "granting" that sends everything into what is "proper" to it.

Second, Heidegger had to expand the insight into the historicity of Dasein that he had gained in *Being and Time* so that it would entail what is now called *Geschick* and denotes the gathering of a sending [*Versammlung eines Schickens*] that has sent itself to *Dasein,* in particular to thinking, in ever different ways throughout the history of Western thought. He had to conceive of the Presocratics' first beginning as such a *Geschick* before the possibility of the *Geschick* of an "other" beginning could become thinkable.

Third, Heidegger's conception of *alētheia* had to develop itself such that it would constitute a "basic trait of Being" or of "essence" (cf. *WdW* 25–26, 140–41). In *Being and Time,* the references to the Greek *alētheuein* and *alētheia* serve only to characterize the way that *Dasein* uncovers beings as "true," by wrenching truth as uncoveredness from *lēthē,* concealedness. There it was shown how *Dasein* is capable of accomplishing this through the constitution of its Being as "disclosedness." This means that *Dasein* is opened [*ist gelichtet*] to itself in its "Da"; it was accordingly determined as a "clearing" [*Lichtung*].

If, by contrast, *alētheia* is conceived of as a basic trait of Being, then this means that clearing is proper to Being itself. Being is then a dimension of openness within which Being's disclosedness or unconcealedness occurs both with respect to the way that that which is present comes to be present as such and as a whole, as well as for the experience of this presence. But since *lēthē* also belongs to *alētheia,* this dimension must also be thought of as being permeated by a self-concealing of concealment, as being permeated by "mystery" and the dissimulation resulting from the domination of "errancy."²

Concealment as mystery and errancy permeates the clearing (cf. ibid., 19–20, *132–33*). The reference to unconcealedness or disclosedness is meant to indicate that everything overt originates in concealedness and continues to belong to it. Concealedness in the form of "withdrawal" holds "unto itself" both that which may never appear to *Dasein* as well as that which may one day emerge. It is precisely this "relationship" between concealedness and unconcealedness that more closely characterizes the way that the *Geschick* dispatches *Dasein* to various manners of "disclosing." As I mentioned at the outset, the *Geschick* of today in the form of the "*Gestell*" dispatches *Dasein* into the noncreative mode of disclosing that brings to the fore nothing but beings whose way of Being is that of "*Bestand.*"

Yet at the same time this means that the *Geschick* could also one day dispatch *Dasein* to bring things forth in a "creative" manner, in the authentic manner that is contained in the original sense of bringing forth (*poiēsis*). Disclosing could become "poietic." If this happened, then "that which saves us" would arrive and thus the conditions for the sudden commencement of another beginning would be fulfilled. But what kind of *Dasein* is able to disclose things in the manner of *poiēsis*? The answer is: most especially the *Dasein* of a poet. However, for Heidegger it is also possible for the thinker to disclose things in an authentic manner. The reason for this privileged position of poets and thinkers that makes them "neighbors" is that both of them dwell in a special way in the "house of Being," i.e., in the element of language. Language is therefore a further "presupposition" for Heidegger's view concerning the special role played by the poet in preparing for an other beginning in poetic dwelling.

III

I would now like to show that Heidegger conceived of the essence of language in terms of *alētheia* and that it is only because of this specific view of the essence of language that the poet is able to bring forth "the poetic" and thereby prepare an other beginning in "poetic dwelling." It must be immediately emphasized that this determination of the "essence" of language is not meant as an answer to the traditional question of "what" something is (*UzS* 201, 94). Furthermore, wherever I subsequently speak of the "structure"[3] and "content" of language—which is a conscious violation of Heidegger's conception of the essence of "essence"—this is done only for the purposes of clarification. Otherwise, the following discussion will remain close to the text in an effort to substantiate our thesis.

1. Only on the basis of the idea that Being, world, *alētheia* and the *Geschick* "give" and "grant" the advent of that which is present in its presence, and only on the assumption that language is involved in this giving and granting, is it plausible that there can be an occurrence in the entire layout [*Aufriß*] of language that as such does not belong to the human realm. This is the soundless event of "saying" [*Sage*], which is carefully distinguished from articulated human speaking. Both of them belong in the entire layout. Saying "bids" and "calls,"; it gathers in a "word" that which belongs to the saying, listens to it and its world and "correspondingly" [*entsprechend*] brings what it has heard into the human, sounding language. The poet brings it into the singing word and establishes this in the articulated work, in the pure poetical composition [*im "rein Gedichteten"*].

2. The "layout" of language in this conception has the same "structure" as that which we demonstrated in *alētheia*. This gives a first indication of Heidegger's own determination of saying as a clearing-concealing way of setting free (cf. ibid., 200, 93). But there are a number of other indications that the "relationship" of con-

cealedness to unconcealedness is borne out in saying. Thus Heidegger conceives of saying in the form of a "stream" (ibid., 255, *124*) in which everything is embedded that addresses *Dasein,* as a stream that addresses *Dasein* not in a resounding, but in a silent manner, even thought it can be heard in its "ringing" as the "ring of silence" (ibid., 30, *207;* 215, *108*). It is a stream that brings everything into what is proper to it (cf. ibid., 29, *206*). This stream of silence originates in a "place of silence" that Heidegger expressly termed the *"lēthē"* in one recent publication (*ZSD* 78, *71*). What does it mean to say that the stream of silence originates in *lēthē?* It means above all that it has its source in that which has not yet been spoken and must remain unspoken: the "unspoken" (cf. "The Way of Language" in *UzS* 251, *122;* 255, *124*). Thus all appropriating "giving" and "granting" of what is present in language comes from the *lēthē,* from concealedness. The stream has its source there, and even if it flows into unconcealedness, it remains permeated by concealment, the mystery, the "unspoken." The *lēthē* holds [*hält*] and relates [*verhält*] everything that is overt in saying, so that it remains also determined by what is unspoken. This whole movement thus has an *"alētheia*-structure" because of which saying is what gives and grants. This does not contradict the fact that the essence of saying for Heidegger lies in the "showing" [*Zeige*], and that saying's "giving" and "granting" therefore result from its showing. For this occurs only within the "free expanse of the clearing," "in which each presence and absence must show itself" (ibid., 257, *126*). In the unconcealedness of the clearing, showing grants the nearness of presence for the arrival of whatever is present, an arrival that remains harbored in farness since it originates in absence, farness (cf. ibid., 21ff. *198ff.*).

Saying's manifold showing extends "into all regions of presence," as we read (ibid., 255, *124*). What are these regions? We referred to Heidegger's determination of saying as a setting free in clearing and concealing in order to characterize the *alētheia*-structure of the movement of saying. What we did not mention, however, is that this movement has a specific "content." What is set free is the "world," Heidegger writes, "Saying, *sagan,* means setting free in clearing and concealing as the proffering of what we call world" (ibid., 200, *93*). This proffering of world is the "essential unfolding in saying" (ibid.).

Heidegger attempted to conceive of the proffering of world in a very few steps (cf. esp. ibid., 202, *95;* 214ff., *106ff.*). It is said to be the occurrence of "nearness" or nearing that brings the "mutual encounter" of the "regions of the world" (precisely those regions of presence mentioned above) into a "neighborly nearness," the fourfold's world regions of the earth, the heavens, the divine, and the mortals. Since this is also what saying brings about, then nearness and saying are "the same" for him (cf. ibid., 202, *95;* 214, *106*). Saying is the nearing of the world regions and thereby also gives witness to the proximity by virtue of which the poet and the thinker are neighbors because of their special ways of saying (cf. ibid., 202, *95*).

Hence, saying is not only a movement that has an *alētheia*-structure. It also "pervades and conjoins" *alētheia* (ibid., 257, *126*) by nearing the world regions as those very regions of presence from which whatever is present appears and "disappears." In this sense we speak—cautiously—of a "content," but since this content belongs to the granting occurrence, we do not mean the content of what is granted by saying, for instance, the content of a poem.

Can we not assume that for Heidegger this "content of saying" is "the poetic," especially since according to his own statements the neighborhood between the thinker and the poet is what gives the "hint" of this particular conception of the essence of language? "The poetic" would then be the essential unfolding in saying, the "essence of language," and therefore also "the language of the essence" (cf. ibid., 200ff., *93ff.*). It would be so both as the proffering of world as well as the "conditioning as a thing" [*Bedingnis*] discussed in the same context, through which the "nonhuman" word calls things into Being (cf. ibid., 232–33, *151–52*).

But how can this assumption be reconciled with the obvious fact that today the poetic in no way constitutes the "content" of that saying that addresses itself to *Dasein* under the rule of *Gestell?* Only when one thinks of Heidegger's determination of the essence of language in terms of *alētheia*—as is the case here—can one see that there is no contradiction here. The *lēthē* belong to *alētheia* brings about this refusal—which is certainly due to the fact that precisely this refusal belongs together in the fully comprehended essence of saying.

Suppose, however, that the *Geschick* of *alētheia* sets the content proper to saying, i.e., the poetic, free; suppose it is what does the granting. The next question would then be what role the poet and his poetic activity play. Is the characterization of the essence of language given up to this point at all in line with Heidegger's determination of the poet?

Heidegger conceives of the poet, and also the thinker, as "used." What he means by "being used" becomes clear only in light of the determination of the essence of language described above. The poet is "used" to bring the poetic, which is the true "content" of saying, into human words. The poet is supposed to "respond" [*entsprechen*] to this content, to the address of what the stream of saying soundlessly addresses to him. That is why Heidegger has called the poets "*die Entsprechenden,*" i.e., those who respond. They respond not only to the "content," however, but also to the *alētheia*-structure of saying. Heidegger therefore conceives of their naming as a disclosing. They must put what they hear into articulated language. His particular view of the essence of language as saying is the decisive presupposition for Heidegger's being able to grant the poet such an unusual and significant role in the preparation of an other beginning in poetic dwelling for mankind.

If this is the role of poet, however, then we must ask whether or not Heidegger has shown in greater detail how the poet assumes and fulfills this role. Has he shown how its proper fulfillment could lead one who is not a poet, mankind as a whole, to find the way to a primordial and hale, a "poetic dwelling"?

First of all, however, how does the poet assume his role and how does he fulfill it? An interpretation of Hölderlin's words, "What remains, however, is founded by the poets" (cf. "Hölderlin und das Wesen der Dichtung", in *Erläuterungen zu Hölderlin's Dichtung,* 31ff.) led Heidegger to the conviction that the poets provide a foundation for the "measures" for *Dasein's* historical world.[4] "Poetry is the founding of Being in words" (ibid., 38). In giving measures, poetry preserves "what remains" in "raging time" (ibid., 37). The poet then assumes his role only if he serves to give measures. Again,

Heidegger conceived of this activity of measure-giving in terms of *alētheia*. The poet can only take his measures and one can only comprehend this "taking of measures" if it is thought of as a disclosing. This disclosing must prepare mankind's "poetic dwelling."

IV

Heidegger himself appears to have determined the essence of the "poetic" in yet another manner. In the essay ". . . Poetically Man Dwells . . ." he sees the achievement of the essence of human Being, the establishment of his dwelling, in the way that man measures out the dimension of an "in-between" of heaven and earth. This occurs when man looks up to the heavens and down upon the earth. And this takes place not just on occasion; rather, "man is man only in this measuring out" (*VA* 195, 221). This measuring is said to be a "measuring out of man as a mortal" (ibid., 196, 222), and moreover it is said to occur "with regard to and by means of something heavenly." By means of this "founding act," man brings his dwelling in a ground plan [*Grundriß*] whereby this measuring out has its "own meter" and thus its own metrics.

Heidegger called this "founding act" of man "poetical"; and in the measure-taking that is accomplished in the measuring out of man's essence, Heidegger saw the essence of "the poetic." At the same time, however, he declared that it is not man as such, but rather the poet who truly has to take the measure for "authentic building," man's dwelling, and that "primordial admission of dwelling." "Authentic building occurs insofar as there are poets, such poets who take the measure for the architecture, the construction of dwelling" (ibid., 202, 227).

In what does the measure for the poet lie? At first it seems that Heidegger holds it to be God, just as Hölderlin did. In his interpretation of the poem "In Lovely Blueness," which was also taken as the basis for this volume, Heidegger first comments on the verse according to which God is "the measure of man." His thinking is thereby directed to the way that God is a measure according to the structure that determines for him everything there is, according to truth thought of as *alētheia,* as unconcealedness. The poet takes his measure from the "sight of the heavens," in whose "brightness" the images appear to him. However, the heavens' light is permeated by darkness. "But the heavens are not sheer light" (ibid., 201, 226). The authentic image of which the other images are mere derivatives does not just contain what is familiar; it also includes the "image-inations [*Ein-Bildungen*] as visible inclusions of the alien" (ibid.). In the heavens, the "unknown God" conceals himself, and thereby appears "as the unknown in the manifestness of the heavens" (ibid., 197, 223).

Heidegger's interpretations come to a remarkable conclusion here: he declares, "That is why the measure has the same kind of essence as the heavens" (ibid., 201, 226). The heavens, however, are one of the regions of the fourfold.

One must note how Heidegger interpreted the verse, according to which the "heavenly beings" are "the measure" for man, in conjunction with the verse that reads: "full of merit, but poetically, man dwells on this earth." In addition to the two regions we have mentioned, that of the divine and that of the heavens, Heidegger was thereby also then able to bring the regions of the earth and the mortals into play. Hölderlin's answer to the question, "Is there a measure on earth?" was "There is none." For Heidegger this can be explained by the fact that what we are naming when we say "on earth" "only exists insofar as man dwells on the earth and in his dwelling lets the earth be as earth" (ibid.). However, this is precisely what man does not do today. Man's essence, the fourth region, is determined in another passage in this essay as follows: "Man has his essence as a mortal. He is called mortal because he can die. To be able to die means: to be capable of death as death. Only man dies—and indeed continually, as long as he stays on this earth, as long as he dwells" (ibid., 196, 222).

The measure must pertain to this "whole dimension" (ibid., 198, 224), i.e., the fourfold, which Heidegger will later call the "richer" relationship in the essay "Hölderlin's Heaven and Earth." This means that for Heidegger "man's measure" is not, as it was for Hölderlin, the unknown God who appears in the manifestness of the heavens, but rather it is the fourfold. Its essence is "the poetic."

I have tried to show that the "poetic" is the "content" of saying that addresses the poet and the thinker in accordance with the structure of *alētheia* as clearing and concealing. Is it not then also this "content" that is addressed to man as such in this "foundational act" of measuring out, by means of which man brings his dwelling into a ground plan? In particular, is it not this "content" that is addressed to the poetic measure-taking of the poet such that it—the poetic, i.e., the fourfold—constitutes the measure? However, Heidegger conceived of the fourfold in terms of *alētheia* (see above, p. 42), and a measure that is permeated by mystery contradicts the traditional traits of a measure (see above, p. 38). Is the "poetic" a nonmetaphysical measure for Heidegger? With regard to the unknown God who appears in the manifestness of the heavens, Heidegger declares that this is not only a "strange" and "bewildering" measure, but also a "mysterious" one. Did he conceive of this measure in a manner that is exemplary for a nonmetaphysical measure? One would immediately grant Heidegger's point that the poetic has the character of a mystery and as such that it is a nonmetaphysical measure for poetry. But now he declares that poetry is the "measure-taking for all measuring" and that it is the "original admission of dwelling" (ibid., 204ff., *227ff.*). He goes so far as to say that the poetic is the guiding point for all construction of what we build. He demands that we "remain heedful of" the "poetic" for the sake of a "turning" from the presently nonpoetical dwelling, so that this "turning" may take place. "When the poetic comes to pass," then will "man dwell humanly on this earth" (ibid.).

However, Heidegger has failed to show the direction in which the man who is not a poet must go if he is truly to take heed of the poetic in his daily affairs.[5] By contrast, in all of the chapters of this volume I have shown that each person is capable of finding a measure in the experience of his own mortality, and how he may do so, and I have shown that the experience of mortality leads to a transformation within him, to the measure of neighborly love. I have shown how today one can "dwell humanly upon this earth."

Notes

Introduction

1. The term *Nächstenethik* is translated as an "ethics concerned with one's fellow man." The emphasis is on the contrast between a *Nächsten-ethik*, which focuses on the relationships between human beings as individuals, and a *Sozialethik* or social ethics, which concerns human conduct in the community or toward other human beings as members of social institutions.—TRANS.

2. Walter Schulz, *Philosophie in der veränderten Welt* (Pfullingen: Neske, 1972), 185.

3. Ibid.

4. Hans Jonas, *Das Prinzip Verantwortung* (Frankfurt/M.: Suhrkamp, 1979). Jonas calls for an "ethics with a changed thinking" (p. 29); for "a new kind of imperative" is necessary (p. 32). Modern technology has made actions possible that are so far-reaching and has brought about so many new objects and consequences that these cannot be encompassed within the framework of previous ethics (p. 26). Even if traditional ethics, the "ethics concerning one's fellow man" (p. 23), with its prescriptions of justice, mercy, etc., is still valid within its own realm (p. 47), one must now conceive of an ethics that does justice to a new fact. What is now relevant is no longer "the participation in a common present" (p. 23) but rather the horizon of the future. It must also do justice to the fact that the sphere of morality is no longer the agent's immediate surroundings. In place of an "ethics of the immediate and simultaneous," an "ethics of the present," there must be an "ethics of extended responsibility" (p. 63) that takes account of one's "collective cumulative technological conduct" (p. 58). In contrast, I am of the opinion that the renewed foundation of an "ethics concerned with one's fellow man" is not only the condition for the possibility of a social ethics, but also for an ethics of extended responsibility as well as for the acceptance of a "trusteeship" toward nature.

5. Werner Marx, *Heidegger and the Tradition* (Evanston: Northwestern University Press, 1971), 85ff.

6. For lack of a better term, "essence," will be used throughout as a translation for *Wesen*, even though Heidegger intends *Wesen* to be understood in a verbal sense that is lost in the traditional understanding of the word "essence." The participial constructions *wesend* and *das Wesende* are translated as "the unfolding essence," "the unfolding of the essence," etc.—TRANS.

7. Following established convention, a capital B in "Being" is used to

establish reference to *das Sein. Das Seiende* is translated throughout as "beings" even where, as in certain passages of "Concerning the Essence of Truth," this term is actually much closer to that which Heidegger later comes to deal with only under the heading of *Sein.*—TRANS.

8. Cf., for instance, Werner Marx, *Reason and World: Between Tradition and a New Beginning* (The Hague: Nijhoff, 1971).

9. *Gestimmtheit,* translated here as "attunement," is often used in German to refer to one's emotional disposition, but is not restricted to this use and should thus be thought of in a much broader, more basic fashion. It refers to the whole range of one's nondeliberative, in the sense of "prerational," attitudes or dispositions, whether they are lasting or fleeting. The term *Befindlichkeit* is employed by Heidegger primarily in *Being and Time.* Thus we have chosen to adopt the standard translation of the term in this work, i.e., "state of mind."—TRANS.

10. Werner Marx, *Heidegger und die Tradition,* 2d. ed. (Hamburg: Felix Meiner Verlag, 1980).

11. Cf., however, the following works by Ute Guzzoni: *Identität oder nicht: zur kritischen Theorie der Ontologie* (Freiburg/Munich: Alber Verlag, 1981) and *Wendungen: Versuche zu einem nicht identifizierenden Denken* (Freiburg/Munich: Alber Verlag, 1982). See also footnote 20, p. 162.

12. In his dissertation, one of my former students recently addressed himself to the question of measure in Heidegger's thinking. See Raymond Gogel, *The Quest for Measure* (Ann Arbor: University Microfilms, 1982), 156. In contrast to the present study, Gogel has concentrated on Heidegger's earlier works. He concludes that Heidegger did not even pose the question, but that the question would be accessible to one who "thinks Heidegger further," as Gogel has done with remarkable insight.

Chapter 1: Is There a Measure on Earth? The Measure for Responsible Action

1. *Das Heilende* is translated as "the healing force." "The hale" or "wellordered" is used to translate its cognate *das Heile.*—TRANS.

2. Regarding Schelling, cf. Werner Marx, *The Philosophy of F. W. J. Schelling: History, System, and Freedom* (Bloomington: Indiana University Press, 1984) and "Das Wesen des Bösen, zur Aktualität der Freiheitsschrift Schellings," *Philosophisches Jahrbuch* 89 (1982): 1ff. The latter article has also been published in Ludwig Hauser, ed., *Schelling, seine Bedeutung für eine Philosophie der Natur und der Geschichte* (Stuttgart: Fromann-Holzboog, 1981). We are not orienting ourselves with regard to the category of measure on Hegel's *Logic.* We are associating only the usual colloquial meanings with terms such as "quality," "force," etc.

3. See Joachim Ritter, *Historisches Wörterbuch der Philosophie* (Darmstadt: Wissenschaftliche Buchgesellschaft, 1971), 3:289–328.

4. Cf. Walter Schulz, *Philosophie in der veränderten Welt* (Pfullingen: Neske, 1972), 749ff.

5. In his book *Anerkennung als Prinzip der praktischen Philosophie* (Freiburg/Munich: Alber Verlag, 1971), Ludwig Siep has convincingly shown how Hegel made recognition the principle of his practical philosophy in the Jena writings and how he had already conceived of recognition as a normative standard and an ideal in his Frankfurt writings. These thorough in-

vestigations have led us to a clearer insight into the precise structure of the concept of recognition.

On *Anerkennung* (recognition), see also Ritter, *Historisches Wörterbuch,* 1:323.

6. The term *Gebirge* means "mountain range" in everyday German. Heidegger uses it in "Concerning the Essence of Technology" as an example of the way that a word with the prefix *ge-* is used to refer to a collection of singular objects, in this case to a collection of mountains (*Berge*). Heidegger gives the term *Gebirg* a new meaning by using it to note a series or collection of *Bergen,* i.e., "sheltering" or "harboring."—TRANS.

7. Since the author explicitly denies that the primary meaning of *Geschick* is "fate" or "destiny" (see below, pp. 127–28), which is the usual English translation of the term, we have chosen to leave it untranslated. The adverbial form of this term (*geschicklich*), the adjectival forms (*geschickliches, geschickliche),* as well as the related terms *Seinsgeschick* (the *Geschick* of Being) and *seinsgeschicklich* (pertaining to the *Geschick* of Being) will also remain untranslated.—TRANS.

8. In *Being and Time,* Heidegger saw in one's "Being-out-ahead-of-oneself" as Being toward one's ownmost potentiality for Being the existential ontological condition for the possibility of *Being-free for* one's authentic existentiell possibilities" (193), the utmost of which is the "freedom unto death" (cf. 266, also 144, 258, 384). These determinations, which Heidegger abandoned after the "turn," were developed further by Jean-Paul Sartre in *Being and Nothingness* (New York: Washington Square Press, 1966). Having established that human reality is "acting," Sartre explicates freedom as "the first condition of action" (pp. 559ff.).

9. This is also the case in the lecture course from the summer semester of 1930, "Concerning the Essence of Human Freedom" (Heidegger, *Gesamtausgabe* [Frankfurt a.M.: Klostermann Verlag, 1982], 31:135). This whole lecture exhibits a general tendency to deal with freedom as an "ontological problem" (cf. ibid., 215). The "miracle of freedom" (Kant) is not what moves Heidegger there, but rather the "unfathomable or wondrous" fact that man exists as that being "in whose Being and essential ground the understanding of Being takes place" (135). Since for Heidegger the understanding of the Being of beings implies an understanding of the truth of beings in their Being and of the truth of the Being of beings as a whole, the question concerning the essence of freedom turns into the question concerning the essence of truth (cf. *WdW* 15ff., *126ff.*). In the notes to the commentary on Schelling, the following general statement is made: "Freedom forfeited its role *originally in the history of Being.* For, Being [*Seyn*] is more primordial than beingness [*Seiendheit*] and subjectivity" (232, *192*).

10. *Gestell* is commonly translated as "enframing" or "composite." We have chosen to leave it untranslated in the few instances in which it occurs.—TRANS.

11. *Bestand* has been translated elsewhere as "standing stock" or simply as "stock" or "raw materials," all of which emphasize various aspects that are part of the German term. Since this important term appears only a few times in this book and all of the suggestions proposed thus far have serious limitations, we have chosen to leave it untranslated.—TRANS.

12. Not only is the "truth of Being" unfit to serve as a measure; rather,

the "event of appropriation" that surpasses Being for Heidegger is also incapable of doing so for the simple reason that "expropriation" belongs as essentially to "appropriation" as *lēthē* does to *alētheia* (*ZSD* 44, 41).

13. "Decay" and its cognates are used to translate *Verwesen*. Though in colloquial German usage *Verwesen* refers to material or corporeal deterioration, the play on *Wesen* (essence) gives the connotation of "losing its essence."—TRANS.

14. The common meaning of the word *Vermögen* has to do with "capabilities" in the sense of "faculties." As will become apparent in this study, Heidegger uses the stem of the word, i.e., *mögen*, to try to bring out new aspects of the type of *Vermögen* that dying represents. The word *Vermögen* has been rendered either as "capability" or "enabling," depending on the sense stressed in the text.—TRANS.

15. See note 9 to the Introduction.

16. Cf. Werner Marx, *Heidegger and the Tradition*, (Evanston: Northwestern University Press, 1971), 94ff.

17. This question is the theme of E. Levinas's works. Cf. *Autrement qu'être, ou au-dela de l'essence* (The Hague: Nijhoff, 1974) and *Totalité et Infini* (The Hague: Nijhoff, 1982).

18. *Ereignis* in common German usage means "event." However, for Heidegger (who says the word is untranslatable), *Ereignis* also bears within it the sense of *eigen* ("own" or "property") and *eignen* ("to suit or be proper"). Because the word occurs so frequently in the text, we have chosen not to leave it untranslated, rendering it as "event of appropriation." However, the sense of "taking over" that "appropriation" has in English should be avoided.—TRANS.

19. J. W. von Goethe, *Gedenkausgabe der Goethe-Stiftung für Kunst und Wissenschaft* (Zurich: Artemis, 1950), 9:42–44.

20. In Heidegger's later writings "responding" refers to the special way that the thinker answers the claim or address of Being (cf. below, pp. 133–46). In her essay "Anspruch und Entsprechung und die Frage der Intersubjektivität" (in Ute Guzzoni, ed., *Nachdenken über Heidegger* [Hildesheim: Gerstenberg, 1980]), Ute Guzzoni examines how the determinants that concern the relationship between Being and man for Heidegger can be applied to the relationship between persons. However, she has not undertaken to think Heidegger further because, as she writes, the presupposition for that would be a "second turn." Her works, influenced by Theodor Adorno, are in general an independent step in a direction that I have long called for—among other things, during our common work together at the philosophical seminar in Freiburg. That is, they are steps toward a reception of Heidegger that thinks him further. Cf. especially *Identität oder Nicht* (Freiburg/Munich: Alber Verlag, 1981), 205ff., 232.

Chapter 2: The Sphere for the Measure: Surmounting Subjectivism

1. In all cases where *das Offene* does not refer to those *beings* that are overt to man but rather to the dimension discussed in the "Conversation," it is translated simply as "the open." "Openness" is the translation for *Offenheit*.—TRANS.

2. Though the standard translations of *gelassen* and *Gelassenheit* are "re-

lease" and "releasement," we have chosen to render them as "let" or "letting-be" because of the incorrect connotation of "expulsion," which is incommensurate with the term as used by both Heidegger and Marx.— TRANS.

3. Would the same thing not have to hold for the thinking that is outlined in the "Conversation"? Whether or not and to what extent such thinking can be explained in terms of the "regionalizing of letting-be" that is outlined for the first time there is a question that Heidegger did not deal with specifically. In any event, such thinking would be in accord with its essence only if it willed that "nonwilling" that has relinquished "representational" thinking as well as "horizontal transcendence" (cf. 50, *78–80*). It appears to me that this can be said for the first time only with regard to the thinking outlined in the "Conversation" because here man must have attained a "steadfastness" that does not result from the fact that he relinquishes his active role, but rather from the fact that he is appropriated to the *Gegnet* (ibid., 62, *81*).

4. In the lecture from the winter semester of 1934/35 (*Gesamtausgabe*, vol. 39), Heidegger included not only the poet but also thinker and above all "one who establishes a state," who takes the "truth concerning the existence of a people" which is originally founded by the poet and takes the Being [*Seyn*] that is conceived of and enjoined by the thinker, and then places them in the "primary seriousness of what is" and thus brings "that people to itself as a people" (144). "This occurs," he continues, "on the part of one who establishes a political state by creating a state that must determine its own essence" (ibid.). Furthermore, in the lecture "The Origin of a Work of Art" (1935) it is stated: "Another way that art unfolds its essence is the deed that founds a political state" (50, *62*). In this lecture, the determinations found in the lecture "Concerning the Essence of Truth," given in 1930, were explicitly adopted such that truth as unconcealedness essentially involves concealing in the "twofold form" of refusal and dissembling (43, *54*). With regard to the theme of this study, however, it is especially important to point out the role that one who establishes a political state plays according to this view of the essence of truth, for it clearly illuminates that there was no measure for responsible action in Heidegger's thinking. The "danger" in Heidegger's conception of truth was strongly emphasized already in my book *Heidegger and the Tradition* on pp. 250ff and 254ff. This judgment is confirmed by the lecture of 1934/35 in that those in the audience whom Heidegger addressed with the words "the hour of our history has arrived" (294) justified the "actions on behalf of the state" that were taken by him who establishes a political state without any reservations on the basis of Heidegger's determination of truth.

Chapter 3: Death and the Mortals

1. "Dying" is distinguished from "perishing" as "departing from the world on the part of that which merely lives"; this is in turn distinguished from "one's life coming to an end" as an "intermediate phenomenon" that belongs only to *Dasein*, which can "come to an end without truly dying" (247). Further forms of perishing are discussed in §48.

2. James B. Demske in *Sein, Mensch und Tod* (Freiburg/Munich: Alber,

1963) [English translation: *Being, Man, and Death* (Lexington: University Press of Kentucky, 1970)] expressly views mortality as an existentiale, although he intends to take the "turn" into account (cf. 111ff., *113ff.*; 164, *133*).

3. See chap. 1, n. 13.

4. One could point out here that it is extremely questionable whether or not Heidegger succeeded in bringing together in *Being and Time* all the various senses of "nothingness": death, the nothingness of thrownness (=null ground), the nothingness of the projection, the nothingness of fallenness, and, above all, the nothingness of anxiety (as the loss of significance) that in turn occurs as the anxiety concerning death, the anxiety of conscience, and as an independent phenomenon (in the chapter "State of Mind"). It is interesting that in "What Is Metaphysics?" only *anxiety* (in the sense of the chapter "State of Mind" in *Being and Time*) is used to introduce the "Nothing."

5. Negation, however, is but "*one* way of nihilating conduct, i.e., conduct grounded in the nihilating of Nothing" (*WiM* 36, *107*). It is not even the "leading form of nihilating conduct" "in which Dasein is shaken through and through by the nihilating of Nothing" (ibid., 37, *107*). Heidegger grants the primacy of having "the character of an abyss" to the "practical" modes of conduct over against the "theoretical" one. The practical modes include "unyielding antagonism," "the keenness of contempt," the "pain of refusal," "the mercilessness of possibility," and the "bitterness of privation" (ibid.).

6. An aid toward an understanding of this insight can be found in "What Is Metaphysics?": "Being and Nothing belong together," but not in the Hegelian sense, "but rather because Being itself is essentially finite and reveals itself only in the transcendence of Dasein, which is held out into Nothing" (39, *110*). It is furthermore stated that "only in the Nothing of Dasein do beings as a whole, in accord with the possibility most proper to them—that is, in a *finite* manner—come to themselves." If the "Nothing" then culminates in the concept of "finitude" in this way, then one must ask whether this was not already "in principle" a step beyond *Being and Time*. Furthermore, with regard to "On the Essence of Reasons," but also in view of *Being and Time*, one must ask whether the idea of "being held out into Nothing" does not turn out to be a "combination" of the idea of "transcendence," the experience of finitude (in "death" and in "thrownness" as "anxiety toward death" and the "anxiety of one's conscience") and in general the experience of anxiety (the way it is described in the chapter "State of Mind" in *Being and Time*) as the experience of the loss of significance, in which the world becomes manifest *as* world. The basic idea (to put it in the terminology of "On the Essence of Truth") seems to be the following: in-sistence, precisely as such, hides the ground of existence that makes existence possible, the ground of that existence that entails the loss of insistency. Anxiety is given, on the one hand, as the existentially distinguished moment of the experience of "ek-sistence" (i.e., as "finite transcendence"), and on the other, as the primordial anxiety, it lies concealed in the "twofold turning away" that "within certain bounds" is the "most proper meaning" of Nothing (*WiM* 36, *106*). This is the idea of fallenness that, as an existentiale in *Being and Time*, is necessary, as it were. The "primordial

action" or "primordial event" of finite transcendence is, on the one hand, capable of being experienced in anxiety as the "reference that, in allowing things to slip away, refers to the submerging beings as a whole" (ibid., 34, 105); on the other hand, it constantly lies ahead of or behind us insofar as we are "fallen," "turning away," "in-sisting." It is on the basis of this Nothing, through the way it opens up beings as such, that we are able to turn to beings. But this turning toward beings is precisely again the *concealing* of transcendence that requires anxiety as a presupposition for its own becoming manifest. If one follows this interpretation, then one could avoid reifications and still describe the fundamental concepts that are implicitly present in *Being and Time*.

7. Werner Jäger in *Gott: Nochmals Martin Heidegger* (Tübingen: Mohr, 1978), has discussed the following question: Is the way that Heidegger accomplishes the step from Nothing to Being the only one that is possible so that it is thus necessary? His critical answer is that, without any hesitation whatsoever, as a matter of course, and without any further justification, Heidegger takes Nothing to be the Nothing of Being. He did pose the question concerning Nothing but he failed to develop it (cf. 412ff.). Heidegger's question concerning the Nothing refers to Nothing other than Being (ibid., 414) and thus concerns nothing other than the difference between Being and beings, the ontological difference (ibid., 415). Jäger, by contrast, takes Heidegger's determination according to which the Nothing is that which is totally other than all beings in a manner such that he attempts to think this something that is other than all Being as something that is "outside of and next to" Being (ibid., 427) so that he does not comprehend the Nothing as Being, but as the "unthinkable other, as God" (ibid., 447ff.). However, this God is not to be taken metaphysically as the *causa sui*. At the end of his book, Jäger presents ten theses about the way we are to conceive of this "unthought god" (ibid., 445ff.).

In his critique of Heidegger, Jäger apparently proceeds from the assumption that Heidegger identified Being and Nothing. However, it is crucial to pay attention to the kind of "identification" this is, as we have attempted to do—in particular with regard to Heidegger's disavowal of "identity" in the traditional sense, a statement recorded in the protocol of his seminar in Le Thor.

8. If the utmost concealedness is gathered in death, then this concealedness is the utmost among all forms of *lēthē*. One form of *lēthē*, for instance, is saying, that as the "play" of the "resounding of silence" is the source from which the soundless work and articulated language arise (*UzS* 30, 207; 208, 214ff., 106ff.). It, too, is gathered in the mystery of death as the "gathering harboring." This is the very reason why, as is stated in the lecture "The Word," "the essence of language and death flashes up before us" (ibid., 215, 107). Heidegger added the note that this area in which essence unfolds is yet "unthought." Indeed, he not only failed to explicate this relationship, he also failed to make explicit the fact that the mystery is the "saying of the world fourfold" (ibid.) and thus of Being as the essence of the world which is gathered in the harbor of death.

9. In "What Are Poets For?" (*Hw* 248ff., 89ff.), Heidegger spoke of death as the gathering of positings [*Setzungen*] as the postulate [*Ge-setz*] or law, just as the "*Gebirg*" [literally, "mountain range"; also used by Heidegger in

a different sense as "shelter" or "harbor"] is a gathering or collection of *"Berge"* [literally, "mountains," in the different sense as shelterings or harborings—cf. on this point chap. 1, n. 6] into a referential whole. J. B. Demske in *Sein, Mensch und Tod* purports to have found a "hint" regarding the meaning of the expression "Gebirg des Seins" [shelter of Being] here. The determinations in that essay, however, are not of the same dimension as the determination of death as the "shrine of Nothing." In "What Are Poets For?," Heidegger follows Rilke in thinking the "other relation" first by turning away from "representational producing" thinking.

The theme is the possibility of a "reversal of the turning away from the open" (e.g., *Hw* 294, *140*) toward the "invisible of ["what pertains to the heart"; cf. "The Logic of the Heart"] the world's interior" (ibid., 287, *134*). The latter, however, is conceived of as in terms of the culmination of modern metaphysics (ibid., 288ff., 134ff.). The Nothing "in" Being does not seem to be conceivable yet from this vantage point. Death is understood as *position*. It belongs to the "broadest surroundings of beings, within which we can only affirm the lack of protection." The turn to the overt is the "renunciation" of negation (ibid., 279, *125*). In the turn to the overt, death is what posits beings in and as a whole. Death is precisely the complete accomplishment of affirmation.

10. See chap. 1, n. 13.

11. In which sense the mortals, "those who speak" (*UzS* 266, *135*), "reside their entire life" in the event of appropriation that reigns in the saying (ibid., 259, *128*) cannot be discussed here (cf., however, below, p. 125).

12. Cf. Werner Marx, *Heidegger and the Tradition* (Evanston: Northwestern University Press, 1971), 191.

13. Heidegger's new conception of the world contains a difficulty that I feel should be pointed out. On the one hand, the mortals are one among the other regions; on the other hand, they are "singled out" insofar as the world is there for them "in a special way." This could lead to difficulties in the determination of "mirroring." The fact that the mortals are extended into the world involves at the same time their being "singled out" in "recollecting," and this presupposes their capability of dying.

Chapter 5: The Measure for *Seinsgeschicklich* Thinking

1. On the word *seinsgeschicklich,* used in the title of this chapter, see chap. 1, n. 7.

2. Heidegger's "expositions" of Hölderlin's poetry as well as of Trakl's and George's are not *seinsgeschicklich* thinking. This is not contradicted by the fact that this thinking has the same structures as *seinsgeschicklich* thinking, and that its task is related to that of the "preparatory" thinking we named as the fourth kind of such thinking. Nor is it contradicted by the fact that the determinations that Heidegger arrived at in his "dialogue" with Hölderlin were also decisive for his interpretations of the Presocratic fragments, which are *seinsgeschicklich.*

3. The determination "a step back" (cf., e.g., *Nietzsche,* 2:389, or *Vorträge und Aufsätze,* 180, *181*) has the same meaning as "leaping" as a leap away from "metaphysical" or "representational" thinking.

4. In order to confirm the fact that we have concentrated on only a few

aspects of the "truth of Being" here in this context, we might point out the variety of ways it is determined in the "Letter on Humanism." There the *truth* of Being is conceived of as "clearing" (67, *204;* 69, *205;* 77, *211*), and the latter as "openness" (100, *228;* 110, *235*) and "world" (70, *206;* 100, *228*) in its relationship to the "essence" of man as ek-sistence (67, *204;* 69, *205;* 71, *213*), especially the latter's relationship to the way that man performs the "thinking of Being" (53ff., *193ff.;* 56, 79, *213;* 102, *230;* 110, *235*). The truth of *Being* is discussed as the "it itself" [*Es Selbst*] (65, *203;* 76, *210*) and the "it gives" [*es gibt*] (80, *214*); furthermore, as the "claim" and as a *Geschick* of Being (81ff., *215ff.;* 87, *219*). By proceeding from these conceptions of the truth of Being, Heidegger projects an other "essence" of language (53, *193;* 59ff., *198ff.;* 70, *206;* 78, *212–13;* 92, *223;* 111, *236;* 115, *239;* 117, *241*) and determines the task of the thinking of Being as a "bringing Being into language" (116, *239*). It should be noted that subjectivism (58, *197;* 89–89, *221–22;* 99, *228;* 111, *236*) and "metaphysics" (63, *202;* 68, *205;* 87, *220*) are spoken of only in connection with the attempt to surmount the traditional conceptions of humanism and ethics by means of a "more primordial humanism" (94, *224;* 104, *231*) and a "more primordial ethics" (104, *231;* 111, *236;* 115, *239*).

5. However, in regard to the word "truth," see Heidegger's retraction in *ZSD* 75, 77.

6. Concerning the meaning of "poietic" as "creative," cf. Werner Marx, *Heidegger and the Tradition* (Evanston: Northwestern University Press, 1971), 139. Concerning the fact that Heidegger came to this meaning in his "dialogues" with Hölderlin, cf. ibid., 158, 185, 228, 233.

7. Cf. on the following Marx, *Heidegger and the Tradition,* 125ff.

8. In German *Satz* can mean "leap," "jump," "principle," "paragraph," "phrase," and "sentence," among other things. It is related to the verb *setzen,* which can mean "put," "place," and "posit." In this text, all of these senses are at play to some degree.—TRANS.

Chapter 6: The Measure for Poetry

1. Cf. regarding this problem Werner Marx, *Heidegger and the Tradition* (Evanston: Northwestern University Press, 1971).

2. The numerous determinations of mystery and errancy in "On the Essence of Truth" and in "The Origin of the Work of Art" have been summarized and simplified here; nevertheless what remains neglected is that clearing and presence can conceal themselves.

3. Cf. on this point D. Sinn, "Heideggers Spätphilosophie," *Philosophische Rundschau* 4 (1967): 81ff.

4. On this point cf. n. 2 above.

5. In another context, I have discussed the extent to which Heidegger did not succeed in demonstrating what this pathway would be. Cf. "The World in an Other Beginning and the Role of the Poet and 'Poetic Dwelling,'" *Reason and World—Between Tradition and an Other Beginning* (The Hague: Nijhoff, 1971).

Index